TRANSFORMING ESL LEARNING
THROUGH TECHNOLOGY INTEGRATION

TRANSFORMING ESL LEARNING
THROUGH TECHNOLOGY INTEGRATION

Samir Sefain, Ed.D.

ARCHWAY
PUBLISHING

Archway Publishing books may be ordered through booksellers or by contacting:

Archway Publishing
1663 Liberty Drive
Bloomington, IN 47403
www.archwaypublishing.com
844-669-3957

ISBN: 978-1-6657-6767-5 (sc)
ISBN: 978-1-6657-6768-2 (e)

Library of Congress Control Number: 2024922597

Print information available on the last page.

Archway Publishing rev. date: 01/07/2025

Contents

Introduction

The education landscape has undergone a significant transformation with the advent of technology. As classrooms evolve and digital tools become more prevalent, educators are discovering innovative ways to improve learning experiences and outcomes for ESL students. Educators' role in utilizing modern technology to make content interesting and approachable—that is, in inspiring students to create, communicate, and collaborate in previously unthinkable ways—is far more significant. This book delves into the myriad of ways technology is revolutionizing ESL education, providing teachers with new methodologies, resources, and approaches to effectively teach and engage their students.

However, integrating technology into teaching and learning requires checking some prerequisites not only on the infrastructure of the schools but also on the teachers' beliefs, training, awareness, efficiency in using technology, and self-efficacy. Limited access to technology, insufficient resources, and a lack of effective teacher training are among the obstacles that hinder technology integration. Meanwhile, learners' perceptions of using technology and their awareness of the importance of integrating technology into learning are imperative. School awareness of incorporating technology into the curricula, standards they follow, and the school's atmosphere should be taken into consideration.

SIGNIFICANCE OF TECHNOLOGY INTEGRATION

All studies on integrating technology underscore the multifaceted advantages of incorporating technology in teaching, ranging from improved pedagogy to improved student outcomes. The transformational qualities of technology have a major influence on increasing intercultural engagement, improving academic performance, and lowering anxiety (Liu et al., 2018). Abucayon et al. (2023) found a beneficial influence on student engagement and motivation, as it not only makes the learning process more interesting and dynamic but also allows students to practice at any time and from any location. With features like immediate feedback, personalized learning, and immersive experiences, technology has transformed the way learners approach language acquisition (Alkhaldi, 2023).

Technology offers authentic learning experiences, bridging the gap between native and non-native speakers and allowing students to emulate the target culture. This exposure improves the educational environment, student engagement, motivation, learning autonomy, creativity, group work, and personalized learning (Lee & Martin, 2020). According to Regan et al. (2019), computer-assisted language learning (CALL) involves the use of technology to provide learners with an authentic learning experience that models the target culture, fostering engagement, motivation, personalized learning, and group work. Furthermore, the seamless integration of instructional technology promotes the development of digital literacy abilities, preparing students to meet the expectations of the twenty-first-century workforce (Falloon, 2020). The utilization of interactive multimedia tools improves content delivery while also accommodating different learning styles (Han, 2022).

By integrating technology, teachers can build dynamic, interactive, conducive, and personalized learning environments that meet the diverse needs of ESL learners, making language acquisition more accessible and enjoyable than ever before. Schmid et al. (2022) found that personalized learning leads to deeper understanding and improves performance. Additionally, technology enables teachers to effectively address multi-level classes by tailoring their teaching strategies to each student's preferences and individual learning styles, resulting in better learning outcomes_(Chen & Zhang, 2022). According to a SWOT analysis (Strengths, Weaknesses, Opportunities, and Threats) for using technology, there are many opportunities as technology improves learners' engagement and motivation (Mariappan et al., 2022). From interactive listening activities to virtual reality for immersive language practice, technology offers a wide range of tools and resources to support language learners in their journey toward proficiency. The range of language learning support technology offers is extensive, from reading passages with audio to expanding vocabulary with correct pronunciation to tools for checking learners' writing and suggesting formal writing alternatives.

Many theories support the integration of technology in language classes. According to Vygotsky's social theory, technological features improve various modes of communication, resulting in better learning outcomes and transforming learning from a cognitive to a socio-constructive process because its taxonomy includes language, information, connection, and (re) design. Aligning constructivist theory, technology transforms instructors from knowledge dispensers to facilitators and learners from knowledge receivers to knowledge creators (Uzumcu & Bay, 2021).

Barriers to Technology Integration:

Ekberg and Gao (2018) classified these barriers as first-order barriers: a lack of reliable internet access, low student-to-device ratios, infrastructure capable of supporting wide-scale student usage, and second-order barriers: insufficient technological, pedagogical, content, and knowledge (TPACK). Additionally, Honey (2018) differentiated between the external barriers, which include devices, time, training, and support, and the internal barriers, which include teachers' self-efficacy, epistemological beliefs, pedagogical beliefs, and perceived value of technology. Meanwhile, Bernacki et al. (2020) divided the hurdles into human restrictions such as a lack of training and expertise, an inability to apply pedagogical knowledge, confidence in employing technology, and physical impediments to organizational settings.

Rodriguez-Gomez et al. (2018) identified many barriers to learners' performance, including plagiarism, privacy concerns, sharing others' schoolwork to copy, cheating during tests, and the fact that technology may sometimes distract students. Furthermore, the evaluation method does not use technology because of spelling and grammatical checks and the ability to use a dictionary. Students do not have adequate storage space on the school network. Learners should know how to troubleshoot glitches; teachers should evaluate the benefits they and students get from utilizing technology in class.

From the school perspective, school administration should create a trend to foster using technology at every step and deepen the concept that AI advancements pave the path for revolutionizing education and making learning more personalized and accessible. Dorrington (2018) emphasized the high cost of purchasing instructional digital series for each grade level and upgrading this software regularly. Furthermore, developing a school-wide protection system against hacking, marketing, and personal usage incurs significant expenditures that the school may not be able to afford. According to De Leon et al.'s (2021) research, insufficient digital educational resources (DER) provide a barrier to instructors since they must go through administrative procedures to utilize the computer lab and evaluation tools, and they cannot preserve either their own or their students' work. Poth (2019) focused on Wi-Fi's capacity and stability in serving a large number of users at once. A technical failure might cause the entire school to lose access. Bernacki et al. (2020) discovered that instructors lack faith in technology since they feel disoriented when confronted with errors or malfunctions, indicating the need for training. On the other hand, some educators choose a teacher-centered approach, either due to a lack of technological abilities or because digital resources are unavailable in the school, making technology integration problematic. Furthermore, Fadda et al. (2020) observed that the large volume of material on the internet makes searching for specific information time-consuming, especially for teachers who are unaware of which digital tools to employ. Aside from that, some teachers do not teach constructively since some techniques are effective for some pupils but not others.

Teacher Beliefs

Teacher beliefs orient their tendencies to adopt technology in their practices. Beliefs motivate behaviors, and effective acts either reinforce or change those beliefs (Ifinedo, 2017). Xu et al. (2019) proved that instructors' perceptions shift when they realize the additional benefit of technology in student outcomes and instructional techniques.

Hankins and Nicholas (2018) defined teacher beliefs as tacit, unconscious assumptions regarding technology integration and the nature of learning. Teacher beliefs are personal constructions based on experiences that might grow, impacting their teaching approaches and the supporting materials they choose (Jagirani et al., 2019). Similarly, Ndlovu et al. (2020) defined the term as a mix of opinions and values that influence teachers' decisions on what, when, and how technology integrates into their teaching process. Sadaf and Johnson (2017) classified the clusters of beliefs into three types: behavioral, normative, and control, which result in consequences or outcomes. According to the Theory of Planned Behavior (TPB), behavioral beliefs arise from personal evaluations of action consequences and influence performance. Normative beliefs are social support or social pressure that encourages a person to act in a specific manner and is supported by the motivation of teachers. Control beliefs determine the extent of technology integration because instructors have better access to resources and confidence in utilizing technology, which gives them more control over the process. Teachers' beliefs fall into two categories: teacher-centered views and student-centered beliefs. The first type is connected to behaviorism since it focuses on discipline, subject content, and moral standards; thus, the instructor has the power to guide the learning process. The second group uses constructivism because knowledge arises in relevant situations and stresses individual interests, which improves students' self-learning capacities and allows instructors to be more involved in utilizing technology (Alberola-Mulet et al., 2021).

Attitudes Toward Technology

Technology cannot replace teachers, but it complements their role in enhancing learners' confidence, autonomy, self-evaluation, and self-reflection through immediate feedback that technology provides. According to the British Educational Communication Technology Agency (BECTA) (n.d.), teachers' attitudes are the most important determinant in technology adoption. According to Shahbazi (2020), teachers' attitudes, including cognitive beliefs and perceived control, determine what they value in digital practices. Huang et al. (2019) discussed the societal effect on teachers' judgments on the kind, frequency, and amount of technological integration. The social impact has two levels: micro-level, which includes school leaders, coworkers, curricular requirements, and student expectations, and macro-level, which includes the teacher evaluation system and school policies. Meanwhile, low resources can impede teachers' working circumstances and negatively affect their attitudes and interests (Wan & Ivy, 2021).

According to Zhong (2017), social constructions, enculturation, direct or indirect experiences, and/or a series of events, all contribute to the formation of teachers' attitudes. Joo et al. (2018) divided teachers' attitudes into two categories based on the National Council of Teachers of English (NCTE): one perceives the world as unchanging but becoming more technologically advanced. This group of instructors does not alter their educational views but does make certain adaptations to accommodate new technologies. This type of "old wine in new bottles" is curriculum-based and teacher-centered; therefore, technology is used for low-level activities such as replacing printed materials with digital equivalents. The other group feels that technology has the potential to transform the world because it allows students to interact, form relationships, create material, and make sense of their learning; therefore, they modify their teaching techniques to accommodate communicative, social, and technical changes. However, various factors influence teachers' attitudes and opinions, including their qualifications, pre-service training, standard awareness, experience, and affiliations with approved organizations.

Teacher Self-Efficacy

Bandura's social cognitive theory (1977) defined the term as people's belief in their ability to attain a given level of performance, which impacts how they feel, think, and are motivated to behave in ways that influence student accomplishment. According to Gomez et al. (2021), technological self-efficacy (TSE) refers to the teacher's ability to select how, why, and when to utilize technology to improve students' skills. Aside from the abilities that teachers have, TSE stems from their ideas about what they can do with those talents in various settings. Teachers' self-efficacy impacts their desire to implement classroom innovations, be open to new ideas, apply inquiry-based teaching approaches, and deal with a variety of problems.

Furthermore, Hicks and Bose (2019), Voithofer et al. (2019), and Nordlof et al. (2019) hypothesized that various factors influence instructors' self-efficacy, including experience, degree of education, personal preferences, and preparation. Zhang et al. (2021) classified self-efficacy into result and efficacy expectations. Efficacy expectations, which are reinforced by the social and application environments, have a greater effect on instruction than result expectations. Successful experiences and the recurrence of those successes foster a sense of self-efficacy, allowing instructors to actively overcome the unanticipated and inescapable hurdles of digital platforms since confidence breeds competence (Becuwe et al., 2017). Some instructors believe that topic knowledge may compensate for their low self-efficacy in utilizing technology; nevertheless, contextual experience helps teachers enhance their techno-pedagogical abilities, which improves their self-efficacy (Joo et al., 2018). To build teachers' self-efficacy, instructors should participate in a rigorous training program, and schools should provide a welcoming and professional teaching atmosphere.

Utilizing Technology from the School Perspective

School plays a major role in determining the infrastructure needed for applying technology, the budget for buying and updating devices, teacher training, and IT support. Cohen (2019) explained that any change begins with the pathfinder, the leader who discovered new technology methods to improve the educational process, followed by conformists who became enthusiastic enough to adopt and spread the new strategies, transforming the school culture into a technology-saturated culture. Avidov-Ungar and Shamir Inbal (2017) identify three dimensions to the job of digital leaders: pedagogical (connected to curriculum), technological (related to suitable technology), and organizational. Schools should have a vision and a clear plan for integrating technology and share this vision with the teachers because the actual changes start when teachers adopt technology in their classroom activities.

Students' Perception

Teachers should check learners' perspectives on integrating technology into their learning processes to change any negativity. Uiboleht et al. (2019) found a strong relationship between learners' enthusiasm to use technology and their age, background, and frequency of using technology daily. The study found that the younger the more acceptance of integrating technology. Martin et al. (2020) found that learners' beliefs varied more intrapersonally than interpersonally and that their use of technology was associated with their degrees of self-efficacy, self-determination, mastery orientation, perseverance, goal orientation, and failure avoidance. Siefert et al. (2019) posited that learners acquire their competence in a variety of activities inside and outside the school so creating a digital learning environment would enhance their skills.

THEORETICAL FRAMEWORK

Social Cognitive Theory

The theory was developed by Bandura (1986-1997-2001) and posits that learning occurs in social contexts as students build their knowledge through observation and test the consequences of others' behaviors to copy the proper reactions. Students learn more by interacting with society, so technology helps them find knowledge through community-building and re-designing it. The theory's key element is reciprocal determinism, which refers to learners' dynamic interactions with one another and with their environment to attain the sense of control that leads to self-efficacy. Behavior has two components: internal (perceptions, career prospects, talents, and personal interests) and extrinsic (family and peer influence and media exposure). Using this theory, we can explain how learners' ideas, feelings, and social interactions impact their use of technology for learning (Martin et al., 2020). The theory defines the elements of creating a technology inclusion environment as the perceived ease-of-use, and the perceived usefulness, as students become keen on learning with technology when they recognize its value in improving their performance (Scherer et al., 2019).

TEACHING PRONUNCIATION WITH TECHNOLOGY

Teaching pronunciation in ESL programs is critical for establishing effective communication skills, boosting confidence, and guaranteeing learners' successful integration into English-speaking situations, as it directly impacts learners' ability to communicate effectively and be understood. It improves learners' listening comprehension, strengthens other language skills, and expands their social and professional options (Pourhosein Gilakjani & Rahimy, 2020).

ESL teachers face the challenge of learners' mother tongues influencing their English pronunciation, which can sometimes lead to misunderstandings. Furthermore, phonetic rules cannot always be applied accurately in all situations. If teachers repeat the correct pronunciation of words many times during the class, it is not guaranteed that learners will still remember the teachers' pronunciation. Practicing certain vowels and word stress in the classroom and at home is crucial to achieving the best pronunciation. This chapter lists many free, some with subscriptions, and digital tools that can assist in achieving this goal.

Tools for Pronunciation Improvement

1. www.speechace.com Using AI to assess and give feedback on learners' pronunciation. It covers stress, intonation, and rhythm.

2. www.elsaspeak.com Using AI to enhance pronunciation, it focuses on specific areas for development and delivers individualized feedback.

3. https://www.rong-chang.com/ It gives great pronunciation exercises, dictation, a vocabulary list with meaning, and proverbs.

4. https://easyworldofenglish.com/courses/pronunciation/ It includes information on minimum pairings, verbs, special endings, and alphabets. It also includes three levels of picture dictionaries with comprehensive material on a variety of topics.

5. https://www.englishclub.com/pronunciation/ The website discusses each pronunciation term independently, followed by examples for more understanding. Stress is addressed in word form, in sentence form, and in linking. The section on word stress discusses syllables, the significance of word stress, and when to employ it. It also includes guidelines and tests on word stress. Additionally, the website offers quizzes on contractions, phonemic symbols, rhyming pairs, and sentence stress. The game section includes questions on homophones, rhyming, and pronunciation (-ed/the/contractions/ch). The games are divided into three levels: basic, intermediate, and

advanced. Students can also practice pairing sounds on the website, as well as minimal pairs with audio. Some sites have videos to help illustrate.

6.   https://preply.com/en/learn/english/pronunciation It gives some nice videos on how to pronounce certain words.

7.   https://www.lingodeer.com/ (with a subscription) It offers pronunciation activities using voice recognition to help students practice and enhance their speaking skills.

8.   https://perfectpronunciations.com/ (with a subscription) Learners can buy lessons to improve their pronunciation. Each session includes a 45-minute one-on-one online meeting as well as at least 15 minutes of behind-the-scenes work to create student tasks and track their progress. It uses artificial intelligence to deliver a range of activities to help improve different elements of English pronunciation, as well as tailored feedback.

9.   www.fluentu.com (with a subscription) It uses real-world media, such as music videos, movie trailers, news, and motivational presentations, to enhance language abilities, including pronunciation. It uses AI to create immersive language learning experiences, such as pronunciation practice. Users can view videos with subtitles, and the AI system will evaluate their pronunciation accuracy based on their speaking practice.

10. www.englishlearning.com (with a subscription) It is an easy-to-use, interactive tool for students of all ages, from beginner to intermediate English. It is a wonderful tool for helping students acquire proper English pronunciation. The simple and effective design includes various activities for practice with visual and audio feedback. Pronunciation Power uses speech recognition technologies to assess and enhance English pronunciation. It involves a variety of exercises and activities.

11. https://murf.ai/ Text-to-speech. With this app, teachers can import text or videos and choose the voice, pitch, and speed to read them.

12. https://elevenlabs.io/speech-synthesis It turns texts into speech, and speech into text. It translates any video to any language and adds subtitles on the screen. The teacher can choose the voice.

13. https://5minuteenglish.com/ It includes transcripts describing the characteristics of American and British accents, as well as helpful pronunciation hints. It also contains phrasal verbs, slang, and idioms that are organized topically.

14. https://app.memrise.com/ offers scenarios to facilitate learning English translated into 22 languages. It provides videos on different topics, and learners can have a conversation using the same vocabulary learned in the scenario sections.

15. https://www.bbc.co.uk/learningenglish/features/pronunciation. Great tool for each element of English pronunciation separately with clear videos.

16. https://www.duolingo.com/. It offers translation questions from multiple languages into English. It also includes dictation and comprehensive English examinations.

17. https://www.voicetube.com/. Provides pronunciation challenges.

18. https://www.englishaccentcoach.com/ It uses vowels and consonants.

19. https://www.evaeaston.com/ contains many videos on grammar and pronunciation, as well as quizzes on irregular verbs and different endings.

20. https://www.busuu.com/ It includes exercises to check understanding after providing English words and sentences for various proficiency levels.

21. Voice-in-voice typing. Download the Gboard app and press the microphone, then speak to generate text.

22. https://dictation.io/. Great app to turn voice into text.

23. https://transcribe.com/. It converts any audio file into text.

24. https://riverside.fm/. It converts audio into text. A built-in speech-to-text feature makes transcription easy and efficient for even beginners. With Google Docs, learners can freely transcribe audio in several languages. Since the system works in real-time, pre-recording is not necessary.

25. https://voice.ai/. Great app to have real-time voice into text.
26. https://maestra.ai/ turns voice or a recorded file into written text.
27. https://speechnotes.co/ speech-to-text
28. https://speechtyping.com/ voice-to-text-English
29. https://voicenotebook.com/ voice-to-text
30. https://app.notta.ai/. voice-to-text.
31. https://www.englishcentral.com/browse/videos great source of educational videos on many topics.
32. https://lingoclip.com/
33. https://www.descript.com/ It enables users to create their own AI voice clone or assign a stock AI voice to generate new audio from text. Fill in gaps in the recordings or create an entire voiceover from scratch.
34. https://otter.ai/ Users can ask questions and/or say the question, and the system turns it into text.
35. https://turboscribe.ai/ transcribes any file with great accuracy.
36. https://www.pronunciationcoach.com This app focuses on improving English pronunciation through interactive exercises and feedback. It provides focused practice and assesses pronunciation using speech recognition technology.
37. https://www.speechtexter.com/ speech-to-text
38. https://go.parlayideas.com/ It gives the instructor and students the ability to design a roundtable for written and spoken instruction with a wide range of subjects to choose from and debate.

39. https://forvo.com/ Students can write a term in an English dictionary, and the dictionary will pronounce it, provide instances, and read the examples.

40. https://www.espressoenglish.net/20-commonly-mis pronounced-words-in-english/ great listening lessons.

41. Www.howtopronounce.com

42. www.youglish.com When a learner enters a difficult word, the app gives a video with the word and highlights it in the transcript.

43. www.howjsay.com It pronounces the word and turns the text into speech.

44. www.pronouncenames.com To pronounce names.

45. www.promova.com Paid tutoring and private or small group classes.

46. www.synonyms.com

47. https://www.thesaurus.com/. Great for synonyms and antonyms

48. https://voicethread.com/

49. https://www.readspeaker.com/ text to sound, translate, and pronounce.

50. https://www.talkenglish.com/video/english-conversation-video.aspx It has many videos for speaking, listening, and grammar points as well.

51. https://en.bab.la/ is great for a dictionary with synonyms and examples with videos on the chosen word. It also has quizzes and grammar exercises.

52. https://eslfriend.com/ Great source for daily conversations, grammar, media lessons, and business English.

53. https://www.bbc.co.uk/learningenglish/english/
    Great source for pronunciation on various topics.
54. https://rachelsenglish.com/ great free courses.
55. https://eslgold.com/ Great source of pronunciation
56. https://www.vocabulix.com/ great pronunciation drill
    for individual words.
57. http://wordsteps.com/ increases the vocabulary with
    pronunciation.
58. https://www.englishcurrent.com/pronunciation/
59. https://www.bbc.co.uk/learningenglish/english/
    learn pronunciation

TECHNOLOGY FOR TEACHING GRAMMAR

The importance of teaching grammar to ESL students can be attributed to several factors. Grammar is the foundation of language proficiency, enabling learners to communicate effectively, understand others, and develop their language skills comprehensively. Grammar enables learners to construct correct sentences to deliver meaning when speaking, comprehend written texts, and produce accurate written communication (Mariappan et al., 2022). Mastering grammar boosts students' confidence in their abilities to produce proper English in various contexts to prove their professional success. Grammar knowledge enables learners to have self-correction for Continuous improvement and build analytic skills as they have to analyze sentence structure and error analysis (Alkhaldi, 2023). Practicing the form and meaning of grammar is important, so below are some open-access websites on all levels, some with subscriptions, for students to practice at home and get immediate feedback on their answers.

1.   www.grammarbank.Com includes many topics, multiple levels, multiple grades, and quizzes.
2.   www.e-grammar.Org It has great exercises on a range of grammatical topics.
3.   https://www.oxfordlearnersdictionaries.com/grammar/
4.   https://www.englishpage.com/ is good at both grammar and vocabulary.
5.   https://www.eslcafe.com/resources/grammar-lessons/ has great exercises on many grammatical topics.
6.   https://english-at-home.com/grammar/ with exercises.
7.   https://www.grammarbook.com/videos.asp These great videos clarify various grammatical concepts.
8.   www.Edx.org/school/universityofcambridge. It is a great resource as it provides free courses on various topics offered by Cambridge University.
9.   https://learnenglish.britishcouncil.org great resource to learn and practice grammar and vocabulary.
10.   https://agendaweb.org/ has a great source for grammar, videos for fairy tales and short stories, spelling activities, and listening exercises.
11.   https://english-grammar.at. It has a great collection of tasks covering nearly all grammatical topics.
12.   https://www.liveworksheets.com/ It gives many sheets on numerous grammar themes at different levels.
13.   https://www.ck12.org/pages/adult-education/#ESL. It is a great open resource for a variety of topic-based grammar worksheets on various topics.

14. https://ca.ixl.com/ela

15. https://experteditor.com.au/blog/the-30-most-common-grammar-mistakes/ presents the most common grammar mistakes.

16. https://www.englishcurrent.com/grammar/ presents several articles covering various grammatical topics.

17. https://www.esolcourses.com/. It provides grammatical instruction across a range of subjects and levels.

18. https://breakingnewsenglish.com/. Great source of grammatical points in the reading text.

19. https://www.myenglishpages.com. It explains the majority of grammatical concepts with exercises.

20. http://a4esl.org/. Great source for grammar, vocabulary, quizzes, and crosswords.

21. https://5minuteenglish.com. It explains different grammatical functions with exercises.

22. https://www.englishclub.com/grammar/. It covers many topics with exercises.

23. https://easyworldofenglish.com/courses/grammar-level-1/ It has three levels with extensive content covering a range of grammatical topics and activities. Sentences are recorded at every level.

24. https://www.autoenglish.org/writing.htm It has great resources for interactive writing for all levels.

25. https://headsupenglish.com/ It offers several grammatical courses with stories constructed around them and exercises for beginners, intermediate learners, and advanced learners alike.

26. https://www.grammarinlevels.com/ It breaks down some grammar rules into three tiers.

27. https://www.autoenglish.org/. It is a great resource to have a separate exercise on each grammatical topic.

28. https://www.jognog.com/. This is a great resource for all school subjects and all grades.

29. https://www.ef.com/ca/english-resources/english-usage/ introduces a detailed introduction to grammar concepts and idioms.

30. https://courses.espressoenglish.net/courses/free-sample-lessons/ has a great collection of grammar (all levels), pronunciation, idioms, vocabulary, and passages with audio.

31. https://www.oxfordlearnersdictionaries.com/resources/ contains a collection of grammar with practice questions, videos, and pronunciation guides. It has a text checker as well.

32. https://www.bbc.co.uk/learningenglish/english. Great resource for grammar, vocabulary, news, quizzes, and tests.

33. https://dictionary.cambridge.org/grammar/british-grammar/ has a good collection of grammar with exercises and vocabulary with pronunciation guides.

34. https://www.bbc.co.uk/worldservice/learningenglish/general/ great resource for grammar with exercises, videos, quizzes, and reading passages.

35. https://eslgold.com/. Great resource for grammar, vocabulary, pronunciation, reading, and speaking.

36. A great resource for grammar and exercises, accompanied by videos.

37. https://oercommons.org/search?batch size= 20&sort by=title&view mode=summary&f. sublevel=community-college-lower-division&f. general subject=language-education-esl

AI FOR TEACHING LISTENING

To improve their listening skills, students should practice different kinds of listening, such as extensive listening, long passages, or stories, to become familiar with natural speech, including intonation and accent variations. Intensive listening focuses on short audio to get specific details and responsive listening to respond appropriately in real-time conversation. Selective listening, in which learners listen for keywords and specific information like the weather forecast, interactive listening, group discussion, and debates, improves conversational fluency. Dictogloss listening, in which listeners reconstruct in writing what they heard to practice summarization and note-taking skills, can benefit from integrating technology that allows them to access a vast array of audio-visual content to create an engaging learning environment (Li, 2023). In addition to podcasts and audiobooks, technology offers many language-learning apps that teach English through games.

Technology offers not only online courses such as Coursera, EdX, and Udemy, taught by native speakers and experts, but it also has online communities through which learners can connect with native speakers. In addition to virtual reality (VR) and augmented reality (AR), there is an immense environment for learners to practice listening and foster their contextual understanding. Furthermore, technology presents smart speakers and IoT devices like Google Home and Amazon Echo that enable learners to interact with devices using voice commands. By engaging in real-time conversations with virtual chatbots, learners can be exposed to different accents, speech patterns, and vocabulary, helping them become more familiar with natural English language usage (Curran et al., 2019). These tools can facilitate the creation of personalized and interactive educational content, cater to diverse learning styles, and foster independent inquiry among students. However, the implementation of these technologies should be thoughtful and considerate of potential challenges (Jia et al., 2022). Below are some useful digital tools to fulfill this target.

1. https://en.islcollective.com/ Offers videos on many grammatical topics and general topics.
2. https://eslvideo.com great video with questions on it.
3. https://agendaweb.org/listening-exercises.html great source with a dictation feature.
4. https://bookbox.com/ very nice videos for short stories.
5. https://www.rosettastone.com/ follows a dynamic immersion method to acquire language through real-world images, written words, and native-speaker audio.

6. https://ed.ted.com/ has a great collection of videos on various topics.

7. https://artsandculture.google.com/ is a great VR app that takes students on a tour of different places.

8. https://www.mondly.com/vr With a subscription, students can take a tour of many places.

9. https://www.engvid.com/ great videos on many topics at all levels.

10. https://eslcorner.settlement.org/ is useful for newcomers as it provides settlement topics.

11. https://edu.gcfglobal.org/en/learning-tips provides some free listening tips.

12. https://highered.mheducation.com/sites/007332860x/student_view0/ great source for listening to different topics. It also has speaking exercises.

13. https://www.liveworksheets.com/worksheets/language/en/subject/english-second-language-esl-1061958 great collections for listening.

14. https://www.excellentesl4u.com/ has a collection of listening for beginners on different topics.

15. https://listeninenglish.com/ has a great collection of listening comprehension.

16. https://lingoclip.com/

17. https://esl.bowvalleycollege.ca/listen/mp3/ great source for listening with exercises on different topics for all levels.

18. https://www.esl-lounge.com/student/index.php provides listening, reading, and grammar.

19. https://www.dailyesl.com/ has a great collection of listening for different levels with questions on them.

20. https://www.englishexpress.com.au/bw great collection of listening for beginners.

21. https://www.ezslang.com/ nice collection of different topics.

22. https://www.trainyouraccent.com/ great collection of different topics with exercises.

23. https://www.languageguide.org/english/vocabulary/ is great for beginners to teach the basic vocabulary required.

24. https://elt.oup.com/student/headway/?cc=us&sel Language=en great source for different topics with videos.

25. https://elt.oup.com/student/englishfile/?cc=us&sel Language=en great collection on listening, grammar, vocabulary practice, and videos.

26. https://elt.oup.com/student/solutions/?cc=us&sel Language=en great listening topics at all levels.

27. https://eduteach.es/. It has videos on various topics and grammar. It has great collections of videos on so many topics, including speaking topics, listening, idioms, and much more.

28. https://www.esl-lab.com/ is great for listening skills.

29. https://edu.gcfglobal.org/en/access/ It provides learners with a list of topics, and upon choosing the topic, several YouTube videos appear to explain the chosen topics.

30. https://www.dailyesl.com/community/ is great for expressing and listening to various community topics.

31. https://elllo.org/video/index.htm offers many listening videos on various topics for more practice.

32. https://calp.ca/express/articles offers many topics on three levels.

33. https://eslcorner.settlement.org/wp-content/activities/ provides great listening practice with follow-up exercises.

34. https://www.onestopenglish.com/. It has a nice collection of reading, grammar, listening, vocabulary, and games on all levels. It also has materials for the IELTS and TOEFL.

35. https://www.esolcourses.com/. Different videos with questions

36. https://www.real-english.com/ has a lot of videos on different topics for beginners, intermediate, and upper-intermediate learners.

37. https://eltpodcast.com/. Different topics and different levels.

38. https://ameponline.homeaffairs.gov.au/mod/page/view.php?id=84 has nice collections on listening and speaking skills for beginners.

39. https://www.learner.org/ is great as it has podcasts, different videos on various levels, and a spelling bee on many levels.

40. https://breakingnewsenglish.com/. It has five levels of speed: listening to 20 questions, listening and spelling, and dictation.

41. https://www.myenglishpages.com. It has the great feature of listening with pauses to examine understanding. It provides great features on idioms and phrases, verbs illustrated by videos,

42. https://www.esl-lab.com. It is a great resource for listening to academics, interviews, and life stories. It is also a great resource on English idioms, vocabulary, and culture.

43. www.youglish.com When learners enter a difficult word, the app gives a video with the word and highlights it in the transcript.

44. https://www.rong-chang.com is a great resource for passage listening, literature, and culture essays. It has a great variety of topics on different levels.

45. https://www.dailyesl.com/ great resource for listening to a vast variety of topics and exercises to evaluate understanding.

46. https://www.trainyouraccent.com/. A great listening resource for different topics

47. https://www.ezslang.com/. Great for slang

48. https://www.voicetube.com/ has many topics on different levels.

49. https://www.englishclub.com/listening/. Different people listen to questions.

50. https://www.autoenglish.org/listenings.htm. Great resource for listening with exercises and some videos. It covers various real-world topics in videos and audio with exercises, but some of them require a subscription.

51. https://headsupenglish.com/ has great collections of videos and listening passages with comprehension questions.

52. https://www.liveworksheets.com/. A useful tool that provides listening on different topics with worksheets with questions to test learners' understanding.

53. https://elllo.org/video/ is a great resource for videos on different topics.

54. https://speechify.com/text-to-speech-online/ reads any text uploaded or pasted.

55. https://voice.ai/ Free real-time voice changer.

56. https://ed.ted.com/ great collection of educational videos on various topics.

57. https://www.teachertube.com/. Various videos on different levels.

58. https://www.real-english.com/ great listening lessons with exercises in each lesson.

59. https://esl-bits.eu/home.html provides stories, books, short stories, articles, and more with audio.

60. https://www.americanrhetoric.com/index.htm great collection of all political speeches in US history and some speeches from movies.

61. https://tv.eslpod.com/p/search#gsc.tab=0 Great collection with a subscription.

62. https://www.favoritepoem.org/ listening to poems.

63. https://www.npr.org/podcasts-and-shows/ Great listening with script.

64. https://learningenglish.voanews.com/ great collection of videos ranging from beginners to advanced learners. It offers lessons on grammar and vocabulary.

65. https://storycorps.org/stories/ great collection of stories with audio to each script.

66. https://www.lyricsgaps.com/ is a wonderful way to learn through music and songs that go from easy to hard. It gives exercises on each song to test understanding.

67. https://www.englishcurrent.com/listening-practice/

68. https://www.magnapubs.com/free-resources/?st=FFsite

69. https://www.hotcoursesabroad.com/study-abroad-info/applying-to-university/how-to-prepare-for-the-ielts-listening-test/ provides listening materials for IELTS & TOEFL

AI FOR TEACHING SPEAKING

Teaching speaking to ESL learners is crucial, as it is the primary goal that enables students to interact in real-life situations. Speaking is the practical application of all the skills taught in the ESL classes. However, many factors negatively affect learners' progress in speaking, such as pausing more often, looking for appropriate words to express their meaning, translating from their native language, or trying to build sentences grammatically.

Although all theories state the importance of giving immediate feedback, in this situation it may demotivate learners, so teachers should focus on the major mistakes that affect the general meaning (Zhen & Hashim, 2022). Students should practice outside the classroom more often with native speakers. Since this might not be available all the time, technology is the alternative solution, as ChatGPT can be a conversation partner that stimulates engaging conversations on various topics and creates a low-pressure speaking environment. Technology can create role-playing scenarios where ChatGPT takes on different personas (e.g., a customer service representative, a tourist guide, a job interviewer) to help students practice in specific real-life contexts (Rahman et al., 2024). In addition, technology gives learners the most appropriate expressions and words. Below are some useful websites that help students reach this goal.

1. http://iteslj.org/questions///////// It has a great collection of topics with helping questions to practice speaking.
2. https://eslactive.com/conversation/. Fun topics for discussion.
3. http://a4esl.org/q/h/vocabulary.html It is great to increase vocabulary on many topics with exercises.
4. https://www.eslcafe.com/resources/slangs is great for idioms and slang language.
5. https://www.eslcafe.com/resources/idioms/   is wonderful for idioms.
6. https://www.theidioms.com/ is the best source for idioms.
7. https://www.idiomconnection.com/ is a great source for idioms.
8. https://english-at-home.com/vocabulary/ is good for idioms and slang.
9. https://flipgrid.com/ Teachers can add topics, files, new materials, videos, YouTube, and pictures, and learners can comment, video recording themselves commenting on the topic, and practice speaking so that the group can learn from each other's mistakes.
10. https://www.bbc.co.uk/learningenglish/english/vocabulary

11. https://edu.gcfglobal.org/en/edlall/ provides different topics to speak about.

12. https://eslvideo.com/chattybots.php

13. https://autoenglish.org/

14. https://ca.ixl.com/ela

15. https://www.esolcourses.com/ speaking practice.

16. https://www.usingenglish.com/quizzes/#Idioms is a great source of idioms.

17. http://gliglish.com/ This app introduces students to several languages with flawless pronunciation on any topic they require. It provides several paid features, as well as a free basic version that allows you to send up to 50 messages every day for 10 minutes. Learners can vary their speed and receive feedback on grammar and pronunciation errors to correct.

18. https://app.talkpal.ai/ This program allows you to practice real-world conversations with a human-like voice ChatGPT. The basic plan is free and allows you to talk for 10 minutes each day; premium provides limitless access.

19. https://smalltalk2.me/ This app exposes learners to many topics such as mock job interviews, IELTS speaking and writing simulators, and vocabulary boosting.

20. https://makesyoufluent.com/ This app introduces learners to real-life conversations to improve pronunciation and get instant feedback with improvement tips.

21. https://eltpodcast.com/

22. https://www.myenglishpages.com. It provides useful expressions on each topic, which are divided thematically.

23. https://5minuteenglish.com. It has lists of slang, idioms, vocabulary, and intonation.

24. https://www.englishclub.com/speaking/ It covers the important vocabulary of the topic, videos on it, and practices.

25. https://headsupenglish.com/. It offers many topics with questions to open discussions for all levels.

26. https://www.jognog.com/. The best source as it has all subjects and all grades.

27. https://www.hotcoursesabroad.com/study-abroad-info/applying-to-university/prepare-for-the-ielts-speaking-test Useful for IELTS speaking

28. Voice transcription. (voice-to-text transcript)

29. Whisper transcription for high-accuracy audio dictation. (with subscription)

30. Whisper Mate app to transcribe voice into text. (with subscription)

31. Whisper notes from speech to text. (with subscription)

32. Simon says transcription. (with subscription)

33. The Whisper Board allows learners to record and transcribe their speech. Free app.

34. Jojo Transcribe is a free app.

35. Whisper transcribe. (with subscription)

36. Whisper Memos app. (with subscription)

37. Whisper: speech-to-text (with subscription)

38. Transcribe speech into text. (with subscription)

39. Voice cleaner and AI enhancer.
40. Whisper, do not type. (with subscription)
41. Aiko. Speech-to-text transcript
42. Voice-to-text transcribing. (with subscription)
43. Speech-to-text and Whisper (with subscription).

AI FOR READING

ESL learners have some difficulties reading due to language structure, cultural background, and personal learning styles. Certain factors, such as the complexity of syntax and grammar structures and the limited vocabulary and idiom reservoir that creates confusion in meaning, outline these difficulties. Recognizing words with similar spellings but different pronunciations is another issue (Aziz, 2023). Furthermore, ESL learners are not familiar with the cultural references, and their knowledge background about the topics is not enough. Most importantly, some learners are slow at reading and not familiar with effective reading strategies such as skimming, scanning, or predicting content, so their inference skills and comprehension skills in getting the main ideas and details are hindered, and their motivation and self-confidence are lowered. Additionally, individual differences and different learning styles make it challenging for teachers to address every student's needs through a one-size-fits-all approach. Overcoming these difficulties requires building vocabulary with proper pronunciation, following proper reading strategies to get interactive reading, getting contextual learning, creating differentiated instruction with scaffolding support, and fostering motivation.

Digital tools offer an array of features that can alleviate these challenges and allow learners to access word translations and pronunciations at the click of a button. Capitalizing on technology not only empowers learners to progress at their own pace and receive instant feedback but also exposes them to a plethora of topics and themes across different difficulty levels. Digital tools can significantly enhance reading fluency in different ways, namely by creating interactive reading platforms that provide learners with reading passages that match their proficiency and gradually increase their difficulty level (Singh et al., 2021). Some tools provide quizzes and comprehension questions to check students' understanding and give immediate feedback. Digital tools can increase contextual learning through flashcards, interactive stories, and games to increase the vocabulary of students with synonyms. Other text-to-speech tools help learners recognize pronunciation and intonation to enhance their understanding. Discussion forums and shared annotation features enable students to share insights to create a collaborative learning environment. Below are a variety of resources and tools on these websites to help ESL learners improve their reading fluency, comprehension, and overall language proficiency.

1. https://en.islcollective.com. It provides worksheets on a variety of topics and can be downloaded in Word or PDF format. The worksheets are the latest and

the most popular. It also has ready-made PowerPoint presentations.

2. https://www.thoughtco.com/esl-reading-comprehension-4133090 Nice collection of readings.

3. https://www.eslfast.com/ has a great collection of reading passages for beginners with audio and activities on many themes.

4. https://www.liveworksheets.com/worksheets/language/en/subject/english-second-language-esl-1061958 This is a great compilation of varied topics for beginners.

5. https://www.excellentesl4u.com/esl-reading-comprehension.html has a collection of reading passages with exercises for beginners.

6. https://americanfolklore.net/folklore/esl-reading/ has a decent compilation.

7. https://www.hotcoursesabroad.com/study-abroad-info/applying-to-university/how-to-prepare-for-the-ielts-reading-test/ useful for reading IELTS

8. https://busyteacher.org/ has worksheets for all the language skills, including grammar.

9. https://www.usingenglish.com/ has a large number of readings on various levels.

10. https://howjsay.com/text-to-speech

11. https://www.commonlit.org/en/ has a collection of readings.

12. https://www.lingq.com/en/learn/en/web/library It includes a large collection of readings and allows teachers to import passages from any source.

13. https://elt.oup.com/teachers/insidewriting/
?cc=us&selLanguage=en&mode=hub great resource
for reading with audio.

14. https://elt.oup.com/student/academicvocabulary/
ui/?cc=us&selLanguage=en&mode=hub   great
reservoir of academic vocabulary.

15. https://elt.oup.com/student/insidereading/
?cc=us&selLanguage=en provides a variety of
reading resources, including videos and audio.

16. https://vizard.ai/ video into text converter

17. https://games4esl.com   provides   reading
comprehension, worksheets, flashcards, and a guide
to teaching grammar, speaking, and games.

18. https://autoenglish.org/ has great interactive content
and downloadable sheets. Some have videos of
illustrations for verbs, phrase verbs, and modal verbs.

19. https://ca.ixl.com/ela. All grades in all subjects.

20. https://newsela.com/home/ provides news at different
levels with quizzes and activities.

21. https://readtheory.org/ Teachers can create a class,
assign certain work to certain students, and get
progress reports.

22. https://www.getepic.com/ is a great digital library that
offers free audiobooks, learning videos, and books on
different topics.

23. https://www.khanacademy.org/ offers a variety of
reading comprehension exercises that meet all levels.

24. https://bookcreator.com/ allows students to create, publish, and share their work to enhance their reading and writing skills through interactive storytelling.

25. https://www.gutenberg.org/ has a great collection of free eBooks to improve reading.

26. https://www.oxfordowl.co.uk/ offers free eBooks to improve reading and comprehension skills.

27. https://rewordify.com/ is a great website that simplifies complex texts for more understanding and helps students build their vocabulary matrix.

28. https://www.readinga-z.com/ offers a wide range of leveled books, lesson plans, and activities.

29. https://headsupenglish.com. All levels and all skills (listening, grammar, and speaking). It includes reading sections about the news or general passages with questions.

30. https://www.esolcourses.com/. Different levels of diverse topics with questions.

31. https://breakingnewsenglish.com/ great resource for reading texts with various activities on them. Text jumble activity and spelling features like missing letters, initials, vowels, and consonants.

32. https://www.newsinlevels.com It has a variety of newspaper articles, some of which are current and some of which are old. It presents three levels of articles with audio.

33. https://www.myenglishpages.com It provides many reading passages and is divided into thematic categories. It introduces useful vocabulary and

suggests reading material based on the vocabulary provided.

34. https://www.cambridge.org/ca/cambridgeenglish/catalog/secondary/cambridge-english-readers/resources great resource to download various books with audio at several levels.

35. https://eslprintables.com/forum/topic.asp?id=32378 A comprehensive resource for readings of various levels and themes.

36. https://www.er-central.com/ is a great resource for reading with audio on a wide range of topics.

37. https://5minuteenglish.com. It has many passages on numerous topics, followed by comprehension questions. It also includes subject-specific listings of key academic vocabulary lists and idioms organized by subjects and grouped by theme.

38. https://www.rong-chang.com/. It has several reading passages with comprehension questions.

39. https://www.english-zone.com. It has materials that cover reading, conversation, and listening skills.

40. https://www.englishclub.com/reading/.   Different passages with questions

41. https://easyworldofenglish.com/lessons/ It has three levels of reading, followed by quizzes. All of the readings include recordings and separate the new words to provide meaning and pronunciation.

42. https://www.rd.com/ has some reading topics.

43. https://www.raz-kids.com/ offers a great library of levelled books with interactive quizzes.

44. https://read.activelylearn.com/ It has a large number of reading passages on different themes, accompanied by a reading-aloud feature. The content is organized into categories, curricular sections, topics, e-books, and news articles. It allows users to upload files or videos, create quizzes, and send assignments to the learners.

45. https://app.getrecall.ai/ summarizes online content and automatically saves and categorizes it according to the user's personal knowledge.

46. https://imsdb.com/ covers a wide range of subjects across several genres.

47. https://learnenglish.britishcouncil.org/ great resource on the four language skills.

48. https://www.liveworksheets.com/ great tool for providing reading passages on different topics with questions to check understanding. Reading passages suit different levels.

49. https://literacyideas.com/writing/ It teaches learners about several sorts of readings, including cause and effect, compare and contrast, facts and views, inferences, and critical thinking readings.

50. http://www.manythings.org/ has so many passages on various topics with sound.

51. https://dp.la/ contains about 2 million articles collected from different institutions, making it an extensive reading resource.

52. https://www.ipl.org/. This is a great resource for reading about different topics.

53. https://www.readwritethink.org/classroom-resources/ great collection of reading articles. Some of them have audio.
54. https://edshelf.com/ paid app but has a great reading collection with quizzes and questions.
55. https://www.educreations.com/ It enables teachers to create lesson plans and import videos and materials. It has many plans, and the basic plan is free.
56. https://www.jognog.com/. It is a wonderful resource as it has all subjects and all grades.
57. www.readworks.org is great for reading.
58. www.vocabulary.com/ provides the books required for school-age students. It has flashcards, so learners can listen to the pronunciation and then click to see the meaning at the back of the flashcard. It has a great feature to practice, such as defining the meaning of a word and selecting a comparable sentence that matches the meaning or looking for the definition in the context. Word games between two teams, idioms and expressions (two lists), lists of significant vocabulary, and spelling bees.
59. https://www.visualthesaurus.com/ (with subscription) defines the meaning with examples and demonstrates various semantic relationships with other words to deepen learners' understanding. It also generates lists of useful vocabulary and shows how to use them in context.
60. https://www.livingfacts.co.za/latest-thinking/ has limited passages to read.

61. https://gutenberg.org/cache/epub/61985/pg61985-images.html#aword is nice for reading and has so many useful books on various topics that are free to download.

62. https://eslgold.com/ is a nice reading collection.

63. https://www.texttovoice.online. Type or paste the text and choose the voice to read.

64. https://www.vecticon.co/tools/text-to-speech Ten minutes free a day.

65. https://speechnotes.co/ It allows learners to dictate and transcribe the speech as well.

66. https://www.veed.io/ creates and edits videos for free.

67. https://www.narakeet.com/ Text-to-Speech and video automation.

68. https://app.wideo.co/. Creates and edits videos. A fantastic text-to-speech online tool for free and a professional video editing online tool.

69. https://www.labnol.org/listen/ Great app

70. https://www.capcut.com/ Text-to-Speech

71. https://easy-peasy.ai/. Text-to-speech

72. https://play.ht/. Text-to-Speech

73. https://fliki.ai/. Text-to-Speech or video

74. https://ttsmp3.com Text-to-Speech

75. https://webapp.dubverse.ai/. Text-to-Speech

76. https://app.acoust.io/. Text-to-Speech

77. https://speechgen.io/ Text-to-speech

78. https://inforobo.com/ Text-to-Speech

79. https://genny.lovo.ai/. Text- to-Speech

80. https://smallseotools.com/ Text-to-Speech

81. https://elevenlabs.io/text-to-speech Text-to-Speech
82. https://www.naturalreaders.com/online/ Text-to-Speech.
83. https://ttsfree.com/ Text-to-Speech
84. https://ttsreader.com/ Text-to-Speech
85. https://texttospeech.online/ Text-to-Speech
86. https://seomagnifier.com/ Text-to-Speech
87. https://balabolka.en.softonic.com/. Text-to-Speech.
88. https://www.voicedream.com/ Text-to-Speech
89. https://voicemaker.in/ Text-to-Speech
90. https://ttsmaker.com/ Text-to-Speech
91. https://speechify.com/. Text-to-Speech
92. https://audioanything.com/ Text-to-Speech
93. https://wellsaidlabs.com/ Text-to-speech with subscription.
94. https://marketplace.respeecher.com/. Text-to-speech with subscription
95. https://www.captivoice.com/. Text-to-Speech with subscription
96. https://www.labnol.org/listen/ Easily convert audio files into text using a powerful API. Users can translate before generating using Google Text-to-Speech online for free. Download your voiceovers in MP4 format and use them whenever you like. The website has many fantastic tutorials on how you can integrate your voice with other unique tools.
97. https://freetts.com/ It is text-to-speech and vice versa.
98. http://www.fromtexttospeech.com/ great free online text-to-speech.

99. https://readloud.net/ Great app to read text.

100. https://www.wordtalk.org.uk/ WordTalk is a free text-to-speech (TTS) add-in compatible with all versions of Microsoft Word. It has a spoken dictionary to help learners decide which word spelling is most appropriate.

101. WordTalk will be in the Microsoft Word toolbar and will allow users to adjust the highlight colours, change the voice and the speed of the speech, convert text to speech, and save it as a WAV or MP3 file so that it can be played back on an iPod or MP3 player.

102. https://reccloud.com/speech-to-text-online Speech-to-Text

103. https://www.englishcurrent.com/tag/reading-lessons/

104. https://www.esl-lounge.com/student/ has all levels.

CREATING RUBRICS

The use of rubrics provides a clear guide for students to write well-structured essays and allows teachers to evaluate assignments more easily. Rubrics ensure that both teachers and students are clear about the requirements and grading criteria for assignments. They also help resolve any arguments that may arise between students and teachers if students are unhappy with their grades. Writing involves various kinds, like expository, descriptive, narrative, persuasive, creative, technical, business, academic, journalistic, and letter writing. Teachers should create clear rubrics with nuances to achieve the four levels of proficiency (Marzuki et al., 2023). All those rubrics should be different for each language benchmark. However, creating all of these rubrics for all of these kinds of writing on different levels is too much for teachers and time-consuming. Nevertheless, digital tools can facilitate the task by creating internationally accepted rubrics for any writing type on all language benchmarks (Peungcharoenkun & Waluyo, 2023). Additionally, teachers can connect these rubrics digitally to the student assignment to make grading a matter of minutes by just reading the students' work and choosing the level they deserve.

1. http://rubistar.4teachers.org/ creates rubrics on different levels for writing, art, and geography.
2. https://bestrubrics.com/ it has rubrics.
3. https://www.rcampus.com/. It is a very nice resource to build rubrics.
4. https://www.quickrubric.com/. It allows teachers to add the rubric they want and the percentage of each rubric. It is user-friendly and can save all the rubrics.
5. Easy Rubric app (download for free) and watch the videos on this link for more illustrations on how to use it.https://thepegeek.com/2018/08/the-ultimate-rubric-app/ This app is versatile and user-friendly, designed to minimize the time and effort involved in assessing students of all ages, levels, and learning environments. This app enables users to create or import their class lists and/or rubrics, assess learners against certain criteria, and generate reports that can be edited, exported, printed, and archived.
6. Easy Rubric makes it possible for students to share their input on designing the evaluation criteria, so it creates a learner-centered environment in the classroom.
7. The **Rubric Scorer app** can be downloaded for free and enables teachers to either use the ready-made rubrics or create new ones. There is a YouTube instructional included with the application.

8. https://additioapp.com/en/rubrics/ With a small annual subscription, teachers can have unlimited rubrics.

9. https://www.superrubric.com/. It has many templates for teachers to choose from– ready-made rubrics or create new rubrics.

10. https://rubric-maker.com/ It has the same features.

11. https://www.briskteaching.com/ai-tools-for-teachers is a great resource for teachers to add rubrics.

12. OrangeSlice: Teacher Rubric is a Google add-on that makes grading productive and professional. Teachers create, distribute, and receive submitted assignments from students through Google Classroom, and Teacher Rubric facilitates the grading process. The rubrics appear in the right half of the Google Docs document to be assessed, and the final grade is a few clicks away. For a more explanation of how to use these apps, see this video: https://m.youtube.com/watch?v=e8050mB5PFA

    a. This tool enables teachers to provide objective feedback to all students while maintaining a consistent grading process. This add-on assists teachers in the grading process whenever an assignment is accessed. Initially, teachers have to decide whether to use descending or ascending performance level progression, followed by standard scoring (A, B, C, D, E, F), or to construct a new rating. Before developing the rubric, teachers must select the categories to be evaluated or create new ones.

b.   Educators can change the final score by selecting the options "extra credit," "late penalty," or "plagiarized penalty" and then automatically process and insert the grade details into the students' Google Docs assignment, where they can see how they were evaluated in detail. They can also generate holistic and analytical rubrics for a better understanding of student achievements.

13.   https://docs.google.com/document/d/1nE0Qy DjmOGPi9ue_o7C_gzqBxlucGA7vRg3ZN18KoRM/ edit#! to create rubrics as add-on Google Docs. The following video explains how to do so.

14.   https://www.youtube.com/watch?v=5NCEP8Gry90

15.   https://chromewebstore.google.com/detail/ goobric-web-app-launcher/cepmakjlanepojocakadf pohnhhalfol

With this extension, teachers can use the Doctopus add-on for Google Sheets to access the Goobric online app, an assessment tool based on rubrics. The Goobric web application allows for flexible and effective rubric-based grading of Google Drive resources (documents, presentations, spreadsheets, folders, etc.) when used in conjunction with the Doctopus add-on for Google Sheets. Teachers can access Doctopus to manage and distribute assignments from any Google Sheet by selecting it from the add-on menu. Simply search for "Doctopus" in the add-on store.

Teachers can access a convenient assessment toolbar, which includes a clickable scoring tool linked to any grid-style rubric, comments, and audio remarks recorded, in the same browser tab as the Google Drive assignment being reviewed. This is made possible via the Goobric online app. The results of submissions can be automatically emailed to students or copied at the bottom of a Google document, and they are automatically transferred to the Google Sheet that holds your assignment roster.

AI FOR WRITING IMPROVEMENTS

There are a lot of factors to consider during the writing process, such as the purpose of the essay, the audience, the paragraph formats and structures, and following certain rubrics. Also, learners must pay attention to grammar, word choice, genre, and punctuation. As a result, improving writing is a long process, and teachers should scrutinize learners' writing, which might demotivate learners who have to take care of so many elements while writing. Correcting learners' writing can be time-consuming and exhausting. Although technology can be used to cut corners, it gives learners immediate feedback to correct mistakes and suggestions on how to improve their writing. Using technology to provide learners with feedback and suggestions saves teachers time and effort. Furthermore, it allows teachers to embed rubrics within learners' assignments to facilitate and speed up grading (Li et al., 2018). Instant grammar and spell-checking are available on online platforms and applications, allowing students to identify and rectify their errors in real time (Muftah, 2023). Writing software with built-in thesaurus and dictionaries helps to broaden vocabulary and improve word choice (Aziz, 2023). Furthermore, digital storytelling and blogging platforms promote consistent practice and creative expression, making writing more enjoyable. Virtual classrooms and forums allow for input from teachers and classmates, promoting a collaborative learning environment. Furthermore, language learning apps frequently feature writing assignments that are targeted to certain competency levels, ensuring that learners receive suitable challenges and assistance (Marzuki et al., 2023). Overall, technology allows for a more effective and entertaining method of teaching writing abilities to ESL learners. Using AI in writing transforms the traditional pen-and-paper method into more creative writing by providing immediate feedback, plagiarism checks, and collaborative editing (Kearney et al., 2022).

In contrast, Peungcharoenkun and Waluyo (2023) outlined some drawbacks to using technology in writing, such as learners relying too heavily on correction tools without understanding their own mistakes. Consequently, their ability to self-edit and think critically may be diminished. Similar findings were reported by Kambouri et al. (2023), who observed that students prefer quick fixes from digital corrections over learning from their mistakes. In addition to negating the learning process, growth, and skill development, this also limits creativity and originality. AI is not suitable for high elements of writing such as argumentative structure and coherence. Furthermore, Reamer (2019) highlighted that AI is not compatible with logical thinking and the ability to connect ideas. Raman and Thannimalai (2019) pointed out that digital inequality might be an issue as not all learners have access to high-speed internet, so they cannot benefit from these AI tools. Privacy issues should be considered while integrating technology into the classroom. Therefore, educators should take into account these potential drawbacks when using AI in writing instruction and address them in their teaching strategies accordingly.

Learners can benefit from the following websites:

1. AudioPen It transfers the spoken text into written text. It can even be translated into other languages.

2. https://app.bookcreator.com/

3. Www.tinywow.com. It creates all the writing components using ChatGPT. The software responds to the title by automatically generating subject sentences, sentence rewriting, paragraph writing, story production, content enhancement, essay writing, and sentence rewriting.

4. Write & Improve with Cambridge (writeandimprove.com) It reviews the learners' writing, modifies it, and offers feedback. On the IELTS level, the website provides several tasks for further practice.

5. https://www.cambridgeenglish.org/learning-english/activities-for-learners/ It is a great source for the four language skills.

6. https://elt.oup.com/teachers/eaw/teachingresources/?cc=us&selLanguage=en&mode=hub nice academic vocabulary collection.

7. Paraphrasing Tool: QuillBot AI This free rephrasing tool will rephrase up to 125 words in a standard writing tone. Premium Quillbot can be rephrased in

the following tones: formal, basic, creative, expanded, and shortened.

8. https://www.duplichecker.com/ rephrases the written sentences and allows uploading a file.

9. https://gemini.google.com/. It is like Chat GPT, which checks grammar and paraphrases sentences.

10. https://www.hotcoursesabroad.com/study-abroad-info/applying-to-university/how-to-prepare-for-the-ielts-writing-test/ Very useful for writing IELTS

11. https://hix.ai/ A premium and comprehensive tool with functions like proofreading, email generation, paragraph creation, and rewriting.

12. https://www.quetext.com/ checks for plagiarism, including AI plagiarism. It also helps with the citation.

13. https://writesonic.com/ enables learners to edit and paraphrase paragraphs, Instagram captions, article writing, and content rephrasing.

14. Www.twee.Com It covers all four language skills, including translation, creating questions, creating a reading passage, making questions on a video, grammar fixer, listening, and many more useful links. It provides essay, article, title and paragraph writing and rewriting, sentence rewriting, Instagram caption, article, blog post ideas, blog outline, business name, slogan, and business plan generators. In addition, it gives a content paraphraser, planner, improver, and summarizer; a content brief generator; a Twitter generator; a tone of voice; a LinkedIn post generator; shortened content; real estate descriptions; cold

email writing; AI rephrasing and detector; a FAQ and private policy; and a poll generator; and YouTube summarizing.

15. https://thecheckerai.com/. Checks against plagiarism.

16. https://hemingwayapp.com/. It is like Grammarly, which enables users to edit sentences or paragraphs, passive voice, and add headings, quotations, and bullet lists. A nice AI proofreading tool with a free trial.

17. https://app.scribbr.com/. It is not open access, but it does provide reliable reports on grammar, spelling, punctuation, conciseness, readability, and word choice.

18. Write & Improve with Cambridge (writeandimprove. com) to improve writing skills.

19. https://www.deepl.com. For highly accurate translations to and from many languages. It offers alternatives to sentences to improve learners' writing styles.

20. https://www.quattr.com/free-tools/ It has several useful features, such as a title generator, H1 heading generator, meta description, content brief paragraph writing and paragraph rewriting generator, content brief generator, paraphrase, summary, and active-passive converter. It offers topic discovery, image alt text, an anchor text generator, cluster keywords, keyword statistics, and keyword research tools.

21. https://www.squibler.io/ai-content-generator This is a great tool for re-paraphrasing all of the mistakes and generating a story from a collection of pictures.

22. http://www2.actden.com/writ den/tips/contents. htm presents methods for combining sentences, paragraphs, and essays.

23. https://www.autodraw.com/. With its ideas and coloring options, Google's tool can transform any crude drawings into professional sketches.

24. https://resumegenius.co. To build resumes

25. https://lucid.app/ generates documents and brainstorms ideas.

26. https://etherpad.org/ is a highly customizable open-source online editor providing collaborative editing in real-time.

27. https://word.rodeo. Creates a word puzzle.

28. https://autoenglish.org/

29. https://ca.ixl.com. It covers all the language skills.

30. https://hix.ai offers content rewriting or summarizing, generates clear, detailed, and instructive prompts, and revises a text for grammar, spelling, or formatting.

31. https://www.myenglishpages.com It covers the fundamentals of writing as well as other genres such as narrative, descriptive, and expository writing. It provides useful links for syntax and academic expressions.

32. https://www.englishclub.com addresses several areas of writing, including grammar and plagiarism.

33. https://5minuteenglish.com. It gives many topics to listen to with exercises.

34. https://www.quill.org/. This is a great resource for teaching writing. It paraphrases, summarizes, translates, and proofreads for grammar errors.
35. https://123grammar.com/ It paraphrases, summarizes, translates, and checks for grammar mistakes.
36. https://worditout.com. It is connected to Google Cloud to create Word Cloud. It converts sound to text and provides captions and subtitles for translation.
37. https://app.jenni.ai/. It edits texts and gives recommendations. The free version has 200 words a day. Upgrades are available.
38. https://app.textcortex.com/. Users can upload a file or write a text, and the app can rewrite, translate, or modify the genre into a professional form.
39. www.prowritingaid.com. It is a great resource that allows teachers to upload a document, and the app can summarize, criticize (organization, writer's voice, styles), grammar, rephrase, thesaurus, structure, and length.
40. Textbuddy is an online writing editor that identifies any mistakes in the text. In addition to proofreading for grammar, spelling, and punctuation, it also comes with AI tools and predefined prompts to simplify writing. Users can write or paste texts into the editor, and it will highlight words and sentences as they type. Among the highlights are excessively long sentences, passive voice, adverbs, formatting issues, and ambiguous language. It assists with flawless grammar and spelling, rephrasing, copywriting,

sentiment analysis, summaries, sentence-shortening, tense-changing, and more writing challenges. The built-in prompts are all designed for simple English.

41. https://literacyideas.com/ is a useful tool for teaching various writing genres, writing processes, outstanding sentence and paragraph composition, editing and proofreading, and how to write convincing conclusions.

42. https://thinkport.org/tps/research-learning-modules. html. Nice source for writing elements.

43. https://www.journalbuddies.com/writing-2/writing-games/ many games and ideas to teach writing skills.

44. https://www.jognog.com/. It is a great resource as it has all subjects and grades.

45. https://www.englishcurrent.com/writing/

PLAGIARISM

Students sometimes use technology to copy and paste from other sites or use ChatGpt to submit error-free assignments, which poses a big problem for ESL teachers. However, technology can be of great help to the teachers in this area, as there are many websites, listed below, that enable teachers to track the students' work and detect all types of plagiarism.

1. https://www.turnitin.com/ Turnitin provides instructors with a variety of tools to help them maintain academic integrity, assess student work, and develop creative thinking.
2. https://www.duplichecker.com/.
3. https://www.quetext.com/. Check for AI plagiarism as well.
4. https://app.scribbr.com/ Great app for proofreading, paraphrasing, summarizing, grammar checking, and AI detector.
5. https://www.grammarly.com/
6. https://www.chegg.com
7. https://www.easybib.com/

8.   https://copyleaks.com/
9.   https://www.copyscape.com/ Great features with subscription.
10. https://www.plagscan.com/
11. https://plagly.com/
12. https://unicheck.com/.
13. https://www.plagaware.com/
14. https://www.plagramme.com/
15. https://searchenginereports.net/
16. https://www.check-plagiarism.com/
17. https://papersowl.com/
18. https://plagiarismdetector.net/
19. https://plagiarismcheck.org/
20. https://smallseotools.com/
21. https://fixgerald.com/
22. https://academichelp.net/
23. https://originality.ai/
24. https://www.zerogpt.com/
25. https://gptzero.me/
26. https://www.editpad.org/
27. https://seranking.com/
28. https://hix.ai/
29. https://plagiarismsoftware.org/
30. https://plagiarismsearch.com/
31. https://gowinston.ai/
32. https://app.passed.ai/
33. https://contentatscale.ai/
34. https://www.paperrater.com/
35. https://www.compilatio.net/

36. https://justdone.ai/
37. https://plagiarisma.net/
38. http://www.plagium.com/
39. https://www.plagscan.com/
40. https://www.plagtracker.com/
41. https://plagiarismhunt.com/
42. https://kci.wrdsb.ca/

AI FOR ASSESSMENT

Assessment plays a pivotal role for both teachers and students. Assessment directs teaching methods and identifies the gap in student knowledge or any misconceptions. Assessment results enable teachers to personalize learning and differentiate instructions to meet the individual differences among learners. It also allows teachers to monitor learner progress to check if they met the standards and achieved the learning goals to set the next set of goals to continue development. Assessment results direct policy decisions and curriculum for the school administration. For learners, assessment enhances their reflection on their learning process and their achievements (Abdul Razak et al., 2023).

There are many kinds of assessments, such as the diagnostic assessment, which decide what should be taught and how, as it checks the previous knowledge of learners to build the new knowledge on and avoid repetition. Ipsative assessment is to compare different results of the same student during the school year to step on the level of progress. Formative assessment monitors every single step of the learning process to provide immediate feedback. Summative assessment that evaluates learner performance at the end of a certain period to compare the results against national and international standards. By incorporating a variety of assessment methods, educators can better address the diverse needs and abilities of their students. Below are some technology tools that can help all stakeholders monitor progress.

1. <u>Create - Conker for AI powered quizzes and more</u>
   It generates essential questions, or "multiple choice, read and respond, mixed, fill in the blank," and can share the test with Google Forms and other forms and tell the percentage of the responses. It accepts any outside texts to form the questions. It accepts YouTube videos or websites and generates questions about them. Teachers can choose a standard and a grade level and can have up to 20 questions.

2. <u>https://autoclassmate.io</u> It provides teachers with 396 AI tools in all categories to match all their teaching needs. Although it is a paid app, it offers three wonderful free apps to use, like *Would You Rather* to generate questions suitable for the warm-up stage and/or assessment for any grade level.

3. <u>https://www.briskteaching.com/ai-tools-for-teachers</u> It is a great source for teachers looking to provide fast and individualized feedback as well as clear rubrics. It swiftly generates progress reports that highlight student successes and areas for growth. It develops compelling Google Slides presentations from

scratch, articles, webpages, and YouTube videos, as well as AI quizzes in Google Forms and Docs with embedded answer keys. These exemplars serve as benchmarks for student assignments. This program prepares students for standardized examinations by generating riddles, question sheets, and writing prompts. This website allows teachers to construct AI-comprehensive lesson plans complete with objectives and activities, as well as generate Depth of Knowledge (DOK) questions to help students comprehend. It also provides administrative services such as writing professional emails, developing interesting newsletters and personalized letters of recommendation, and keeping extensive notes on student conduct and learning progress. It also assists teachers in inspecting student writing, in addition to having translation capability for several languages.

4. http://www.contentgenerator.net/ This software allows teachers to build engaging eLearning activities, such as lengthy or short quizzes and multiple-choice questions.

5. QuestionWell is a great app that can generate text on any subject, create questions, and then export these questions to Google Forms, Google Slides, and MS Word.

6. https://drive.google.com/drive/mobile/folders/14QU2N191byzVgxRDosK1TMYMk8qYkYTG

7. https://www.usingenglish.com/quizzes/#Idioms great resource for quizzes on grammar and idioms.

8. https://practice.accuplacer.org/home/test/3 is a great source of exams for reading, listening, and writing accredited by the Texas initiative.

9. https://testmoz.com/. Great at building a quiz, assigning it, and grading it.

10. www.yippity.io Users get three free AI quiz generations per month. Quizzes can be generated from pasted text (10,000 words max) or a web link. Answers are revealed by default but can be hidden by clicking on the eye icon. Questions and answers can also be pasted into digital flashcards.

11. https://new.parlayideas.com/ Teachers can insert a link to web-based media (such as YouTube videos) and choose a grade level for the discussion questions. Teachers can create a writing roundtable, invite students, develop a question, and set the setting. After students share their writing, the instructor receives a summary of the conversation as well as a performance sheet. In the speaking table, the teacher arranges a circular table, and students "tap in," so the system puts them in a queue and allows them to record their responses. The system subsequently provides a summary of the speech and chart. Teachers may design courses and browse thousands of topics to choose from. Parlay Genie's AI develops questions for conversation.

12. https://quizgecko.com. To build quizzes on any passage or upload quizzes. It has all kinds of questions.

13. https://www.to-teach.ai. Wikipedia articles can be seamlessly converted into interactive exercises for students using AI. Additionally, teachers can effortlessly create worksheets based on YouTube videos for up to 40 minutes in duration. The program boasts an array of features, such as generating word puzzles, matching terms, questions, sample responses, crosswords, gap text, tasks, and mind maps as templates for images. It also offers the creation of multiple-choice quizzes, text tables, true/false questions, and assignments for summarizing, analyzing, and simplifying texts. Moreover, it's capable of generating a dictionary of the text to clarify complex concepts and adjust the text's language level as per the requirement. Furthermore, it excels at transforming any text into a more captivating and simpler format, such as crafting scripts from fairy tales, generating short stories from newspaper articles, or creating conversations from YouTube videos. Also, it provides comprehensive grammatical lessons and activities.

14. https://tools.fobizz.com/ai for all assignments.

15. https://www.usingenglish.com/reference/ great reference for grammar exercises.

16. https://www.prepai.io. Great at creating all kinds of questions about any text.

17. https://minipoll.co. Set up a poll to get learners' opinions about any topic.

18. https://admin.sli.do/. Allows users to create slides to build quizzes, polls, multiple choices, word clouds, and open text questions.

19. https://www.revision.ai/. It makes a quiz on any file.

20. https://www.bbc.co.uk/learningenglish/english/features/quizzes2024 on grammar.

21. https://vocaroo.com/ to record voices.

22. https://en.islcollective.com. It adds quizzes to any YouTube videos with all levels and kinds of questions. Vocabulary or grammar quizzes.

23. https://www.education.com/worksheets/ela/

24. https://www.wordsmyth.net/activities/multiple choice2/ great question bank for matching, fill-in gaps, multiple choices, and quizzes.

25. https://www.myenglishpages.com offers general exercises on many topics.

26. https://www.esl-lab.com. Great source of vocabulary, grammar, and idiom quizzes.

27. https://www.rong-chang.com/. It introduces scrambled sentences to test understanding.

28. https://www.funtrivia.com/ great source for quizzes, games, and different topics.

29. https://www.englishclub.com/ has lists of vocabulary, spelling tests, and proverbs.

30. https://quizlet.com/ca. It creates flashcards for the topic the teacher adds, then it can turn the flash card into a test with all kinds of questions, checkpoints, and games, and it helps learners' study through personalized learning as it is great at vocabulary building and language learning.

31. https://www.equiz.me/ with quizzes on different aspects.

32. https://www.triviaplaza.com/language-idioms-quizzes/ great quizzes on idioms and other language parts.

33. https://quizizz.com/. To create PowerPoint for multiple-choice, fill-in-the-gap questions, and polls.

34. https://www.ego4u.com/en/chill-out/games quizzes on various topics.

35. https://app.quizalize.com/. Teachers can create a timing quiz in a second and games in between each question.

36. https://www.grammarbook.com/interactive quizzes exercises.asp Great quizzes on different grammatical points.

37. https://answergarden.ch/ to create quizzes.

38. https://openclass.ai/ great at building quizzes.

39. https://quiztools.weebly.com/ is a great source that offers various assessment tools.

40. https://www.pollfish.com/ great app for single selection, multiple selections, open-ended, description, numeric open-ended, rating stars, slider, and drill down.

41. https://www.plickers.com/. It is a great resource to create slides with questions about the topics. Teachers can import questions, videos, sounds, and pictures to support the slides.

42. https://www.mentimeter.com/ helps create quizzes, surveys, all kinds of questions, and polls.

43. https://www.cognitoforms.com/. It has a great reservoir of basic, intermediate, and advanced forms on different topics, mostly surveys.
44. https://www.duplichecker.com/ great resource that rewrites the text and checks for grammar mistakes, plagiarism, and vocabulary synonyms.
45. https://admin.typeform.com/ allows users to create exams.
46. https://www.schrockguide.net/digital-storytelling.html
47. https://www.sherstonamerica.com/eassessment/ e-assessment (with subscription).
48. https://www.jognog.com/. is a great source as it has all subjects and all grades.
49. https://edpuzzle.com/ has some videos with pauses to question learners.
50. http://quizstar.4teachers.org/
51. https://quizbot.ai/ creates questions (all types) from video, pictures, audio, and files, checks for plagiarism, and rewrites sentences (with subscription).
52. http://persuadestar.4teachers.org/.   Creates assignments and assigns students to them.
53. http://trackstar.4teachers.org/
54. http://assignaday.4teachers.org/.
55. http://casanotes.4teachers.org/
56. http://pblchecklist.4teachers.org/
57. http://notestar.4teachers.org/
58. http://thinktank.4teachers.org/

59. https://suite.smarttech-prod.com/. It is great for creating slides and a library, and it allows teachers to import from external sources.

60. http://www.edtechroundup.org/reviews/quizbean-the-online-quiz-creator

61. https://quiztools.weebly.com/

62. https://www.classmarker.com/online-exam-software/ Creates and gives exams and gives results.

63. https://edshelf.com/tool/kubbu/

64. https://questbase.com/en/

65. https://www.questgen.ai/ generates quizzes from video or audio. Generates quizzes from any image, snapshot, or uploaded file (with subscription).

66. https://kahoot.com/ Known for its engaging and game-like quizzes, Kahoot! allows teachers to create interactive quizzes that students can participate in using any device. It's great for real-time assessment and feedback.

67. https://padlet.com/. While not a traditional quiz or assessment tool, Padlet offers unique ways to gather student responses and insights. It's an interactive bulletin board where students can post text, images, links, and more.

68. https://seesaw.com/ Ideal for younger students, Seesaw provides a student-driven digital portfolio platform where students can submit their work and teachers can provide feedback.

69. https://b.socrative.com/. A real-time assessment tool that provides quizzes, quick question polls, exit tickets,

and space races. Socrative is known for its simplicity and effectiveness in classroom engagement.

70. https://app.formative.com/ This tool allows teachers to create assignments and assessments that students can answer in real time. It offers a variety of question types and real-time feedback features.

71. https://www.fillout.com/ai-quiz-maker great at creating quizzes on any passage.

72. https://www.revisely.com/quiz-generator. A quiz maker, but with a subscription.

73. https://app.schoology.com/ A comprehensive learning management system that offers assessment management, collaborative tools, and a platform for curriculum building.

74. https://www.mentimeter.com/ to build open-ended questions or PPTs.

75. https://www.flexiquiz.com/. To build quizzes with different types of questions: multiple choices, open-ended, matching, and fill-in gaps.

76. https://www.baamboozle.com/ also to build a test.

77. https://www.sporcle.com/ for quiz building.

78. https://presenter.ahaslides.com/. Quiz building.

79. https://www.usingenglish.com/ has a lot of quizzes on grammar and vocabulary.

80. https://englishteststore.net/. Great source of question bank on all language skills.

81. https://englishpracticetest.net/. A great source with a wonderful question bank on all language skills and all levels.

82. https://test-english.com/
83. https://agendaweb.org/ great source with a good reservoir of exercises on grammar, listening, vocabulary, reading, and quizzes.
84. https://english.best/tests/toeic English for high level.
85. http://www.pearltrees.com/u/621754-english-tests-toeflr-toeicr To practice high level English
86. https://www.academia.edu/4865167/ 2003 2006 www english test net. = https://bouraoui1belhadef. wordpress.com/wp-content/uploads/2011/01/ d8aad985d8a7d8b1d98ad986-d984d8bad8a9-d8a5d986d8acd984d98ad8b2d98ad8a9-d985d8b9-d8a7d984d8add984d988d984.pdf These two references have a great question bank on all grammar points with answer key.
87. https://testyourenglish.net/toefl/toefl practice tests. html High level English
88. https://testyourenglish.net/english-online/menu/ comprehension-tests.html
89. https://www.examsnet.com/competitive-english-practice-tests. Great, actual exam with timing.
90. https://www.cambridgeenglish.org/test-your-english/
91. https://www.ownexams.com/exam-university? p0=1471
92. https://www.englishtestsonline.com/english-grammar-tests/ has nice questions about grammar, vocabulary.
93. https://www.englishcurrent.com/exercises/
94. https://www.englishcurrent.com/free-english-tests/

95. https://www.esl-lounge.com/student/ has all levels.

96. Interactive Quizzes and Games: Develop interactive quizzes and language learning games powered by ChatGPT. For example, learners can play word association games, fill-in-the-blank exercises, or trivia quizzes where ChatGPT generates questions and evaluates responses.

AI FOR GRADING

1. https://www.gradescope.com. Free trial for two weeks. Teachers can upload all the materials, and the website can build the exam and then grade it.

2. https://app.essaygrader.ai It is a great app for grading essays with ready-made rubrics and allows you to have your rubrics. It gives detailed feedback. It also has the feature of summarizing any text. Students can use it before submission.

3. https://tools.fobizz.com/ai It gives automated grading and feedback suggestions for student assignments based on the criteria the teacher inserts. The app will provide evaluations, suggestions, lists of mistakes, and transcripts of the student's assignment.

It converts video and voice recordings into text from Vimeo, YouTube, mp3, video, or audiovisual and uses this transcript for educational tasks.

An AI image generator can turn your ideas into pictures to illustrate them in the classroom, using multiple versions and themes in different styles to create discussions among students.

AI PDF chat can summarize a PDF document, create question-answer pairs for flashcards, or provide answers to questions about its content.

AI worksheets for practice as it creates, shares, and evaluates them online by creating different types of tasks. Learners share it via a link or QR code and evaluate the results. It can create fun digital sheets, forms, and questionnaires and review the results. It enables teachers to create and share digital quizzes and exercises and collect results. Additionally, it tests learners' prior knowledge and lets them share opinions and self-assessments.

It generates a board with assignments for your students to choose from using an anagram (an anagram is a word or phrase formed by rearranging the letters of a different word or phrase). It is scrambled versions of some words, while the task is to unscramble these words. It has exercises to practice vocabulary and spelling. For best practice examples and solutions, it creates model solutions for your students for successful task completion with methodological annotations and explanations.

As for classroom discussion, it generates inspiring teacher notes and ideas for captivating classroom conversations. Additionally, it explores the most common misconceptions students have about a specific topic and learns how to address them. If the teacher is creating a course syllabus, it drafts a course syllabus for several lessons on a specific topic. Also, it creates detailed learning objectives by generating differentiated learning objectives, including a minimum, a standard, and a maximum learning objective. It also generates a gap-fill story with a gap-fill exercise in the form of a short story to help students master new vocabulary and terminologies. With gap-fill text features, learners write a gap-fill exercise in the format of a factual text that will help them contextualize expertise and subject-related terminologies. It also makes a recommendation for teachers searching for personal gifts for their colleagues and students. It generates a glossary with explanations of key terms and relevant concepts. As for grading text, it generates grading suggestions for writing assignments with annotations on criteria like accuracy and quality of writing.

The icebreaker activities generate icebreaker games, activities, and conversation starters. In addition, it generates original academic content and informational texts customized to the criteria of your choice. Key terms and concepts create multi-level explanations for students with different reading levels and special learning needs. It helps in all kinds of formal writing, such as letters of recommendation, class and field trips, teacher-parent conferences, and reference letters. It creates word-matching activities, reading materials, real-world connection handouts, and team games for icebreaking. It can mark, revise the texts and change their genre or add to their complexity. It also creates rubrics, short stories or songs, and quotes of the day and translates them.

https://www.flubaroo.com/ Flubaroo is a free tool that helps you quickly grade multiple-choice or fill-in-the-blank assignments.

ELECTRONIC FOLDERS

Keeping a record of students' work is important for a variety of reasons, including improving educational results and the overall learning environment. This encompasses so many benefits, such as tracking the learners' progress to identify areas of growth and, hence creating personalized instructions. It gives a complete picture of learners' work throughout the school year to have formative and summative assessments and to enable teachers to build constructive feedback and make informed decisions. Records play a pivotal role in motivating learners by setting realistic goals and conducting self-assessments. Administrators also benefit from this record, as they make sure that all students receive all the required support in the specific areas of improvement. Getting comprehensive data about the students' progress enables administrators to make informed decisions on curriculum development, professional development needed, and any policy changes. Additionally, keeping a record enables teachers to reflect on their teaching styles and make any necessary adjustments to improve their practices.

According to the Portfolio-Based Language Assessment

(PBLA), teachers are required to keep a record of all learners' artifacts and skill-building exercises. This means that learners need to carry a heavy binder containing all their language benchmark artifacts to each class, which is both burdensome and expensive. Using technology could provide a more cost-effective and efficient alternative to this system. Below are some websites that help teachers keep a record of their students' progress. Below is a collection of websites to serve this object.

https://www.livebinders.com/. Both premium and free features are available.

https://edshelf.com/provides great free features.

https://b.socrative.com/ It enables teachers to build quizzes with multiple-choice, true and false, and short answers. Teachers can build assessments and reports.

AI FOR LESSON PREPARATION

It is crucial for teachers to be well-prepared before class so that they can clearly outline the lesson objectives to be met within a set time frame. The lesson plan should include the 5 E's (Engage, Explore, Explain, Elaborate, Evaluate). Lesson planning enables teachers to address the diverse needs, abilities, and interests of learners, incorporating relevant feedback and evaluation. Well-prepared lessons allow teachers to deliver effective, engaging, and inclusive instruction, which boosts their confidence and positively impacts student learning and classroom management. Below are some useful AI-assisted lesson planning and teaching resources to fulfill this target.

1. https://www.eduaide.ai/ This tool provides great features for the teachers to build a lesson plan. For example, "Lesson Seed" provides comprehensive lessons that include various activities. Other useful features like Prior Knowledge+ Scaffolding, Engagement activities, Assessment Measures, Learning Objectives, Lesson Plan-5E's, Unit Plan, and Evidence Statements. The tool has saved materials

and allows teachers to paste their materials to build all kinds of lessons on.

2. https://oercommons.org/. One of the best and richest open sources to get materials for all the language skills with exercises and accompanied by videos for more illustration.

3. https://app.schoolai.com/. It is a free app for teachers and has so many features, like generating and modifying comprehensive lesson plans, multiple-choice quizzes on any topic, generating rubrics for assignments, worksheets on any topic, customizable jokes to engage students, vocabulary lists, generating letters of recommendation, and text translation.

4. https://www.pbslearningmedia.org/ is great at building lessons and providing all the needed materials and tools.

5. https://www.slideshare.net

6. https://www.chatba.com/ It turns any topic into slides to facilitate the presentation.

7. https://www.lessonplanet.com/ Great paid app with all the required materials.

8. https://educators.brainpop.com/ Good source

9. https://lcc.issbc.org/ Premium products are great.

10. https://www.kids.niehs.nih.gov/topics has great topics for beginners.

11. https://www.thoughtco.com/esl-4133095 is a great open source for pronunciation, videos, grammar, vocabulary, business idioms, business writing, and reading passages.

12. https://h5p.org/node/1037876 offers great features with a monthly subscription. Its features include a title slide, an instruction slide, an activity summary slide, hyperlinks, Twitter feeds, and mixed media, including video, audio, animation, and images. In addition, it has great interactive questioning activities such as fill-in-the-blanks, multiple-choice, single-choice, and drag-and-drop text and/or images. The app has the feature of asking users to select the best summary, mark the words, use dialogue cards, and watch interactive videos.

13. https://wordsift.org/ turns sentences into a word cloud, pictures, and/or video.

14. https://www.visualthesaurus.com/dictionary with word cloud features

15. https://www.cram.com/ offers quizzes, flashcards, essay writing, and a check for plagiarism.

16. https://queensu.thinkific.com/ It offers free English courses for beginners in six modules.

17. https://app.popplet.com creates a mind map.

18. https://www.slidescarnival.com/. Exports to PPT

19. https://sway.cloud.microsoft.com/my is one of the greatest presentation tools, with a plethora of features. It is more professional than PowerPoint.

20. https://www.haikudeck.com/ It enables teachers to create power points 20 times faster and more professionally due to the great reservoir of galleries and features.

21. https://learningpool.com/

22. https://elt.oup.com/learning_resources/?cc=us&sel Language=en&mode=hub great comprehensive source for different topics with pronunciation and audio.

23. https://www.plickers.com/ great app for skill building and a question bank with the ability to insert pictures.

24. https://app.peardeck.com/= https://app.edulastic.com/author/dashboard. to create lessons or use stored ones.

25. https://nearpod.com/ has a library and videos to use. It also has options to upload lessons, questions, and interactive videos.

26. https://www.learner.org/. Has many podcasts

27. https://m.youtube.com/watch?v=NIgSFEb4H9Q This link explains how to use NearPod features.

28. https://www.classpoint.io/pric Create an interactive PowerPoint or poll.

29. https://classflow.com/ Great features for lesson delivery

30. https://www.iorad.com/pl This is a tutorial video to explain how to use the class flow features.

31. https://suite.smarttech-prod.com/ is a great lesson delivery platform with a nice library and options to upload PDF files or videos to the lesson.

32. https://helpmeteach.ai/ Nice features to deliver materials (with subscription).

33. https://app.classkick.com It is great for creating lessons, assignments, and quizzes.

34. https://padlet.com. Great for presentation

35. https://www.polleverywhere.com/ To create a poll, PowerPoint, or other products.

36. https://gamma.app/. Creates PPT and can import or export any theme with pictures.

37. https://www.lessonplans.ai/.

38. https://www.lessonup.com/. It is great to build up the lesson and gather the contents the teacher likes. It has a great reservoir of lessons using PPT and videos.

39. https://fluentkey.com/. Like a lesson up, but free.

40. https://www.teach-anything.com/ It gives answers to any question, and the user can use the level of proficiency of the answer.

41. https://www.perplexity.ai/ It is like ChatGpt that answers questions but this website gives the users the source of the answers.

42. https://educationcopilot.com/

43. https://www.roshi.ai/how-to. It creates a lesson from YouTube or loaded text or audio.

44. https://curipod.com. This websites provides a good collection of lesson planning on many topics for teachers to choose from.

45. https://www.thinglink.com/ creates content to present, interact with, and give a learning experience.

46. https://www.goconqr.com/ To create the course contents with the library.

47. https://minicoursegenerator.com. helps teachers create their courses.

48. https://www.readwritethink.org/classroom-resources/lesson-plans/ Nice collection of articles.

49. https://bogglesworldesl.com/ has a great collection as it provides teachers with different topics on elementary, intermediate, and advanced levels and builds crosswords, word searches, flashcards, songs, creative writing, games, and worksheets on the topic. It also has a writer's workshop, creative writing, pronunciation, videos, and many ESL articles.

50. https://www.ef.com/wwen/english-resources/ is great for grammar, idioms, vocabulary, and level tests.

51. https://www.bbc.co.uk/bitesize/ This websites provides lesson plans for all subjects and all grades.

52. https://www.bbc.co.uk/worldservice/learningenglish/general/ has wonderful collections of videos, quizzes, and grammar.

53. https://classroomscreen.com/. It enables users to choose a background and add voice or text to it.

54. Google also offers some tools teachers can use to present their lessons professionally.

55. Google Classroom provides both teachers and students with a complete educational platform, free to use. Teachers can assign homework, correct it against certain rubrics, and follow the progress of each student.

56. Google Duo: It benefits online classes by enabling high-quality video calls that are end-to-end encrypted. A teacher can create a group to answer the questions of each student and personalize the learning process.

57. Google Docs offers a "Share" feature that enables the teacher to share the same page that each student is writing to give instant feedback.

58. Google Collection provides teachers with the feature to collect and sort out the materials to be used according to the skill and the learners' levels. This video explains the process of using this app. https://www.youtube.com/watch?v=IXlTpR0tOfc

59. Google Sheets lets users create and collaborate on online spreadsheets in real time, which is useful for keeping a record of each student's exams and attendance.

60. Google Jam board (for drawing) A collaborative digital whiteboard that enables learners to engage from anywhere and can pull in images and use easy-to-read handwriting. It unleashes students' creativity and allows for easy sharing or making real-world connections, so it gives each student a voice regardless of their level. This video explains how to use it. https://edu.google.com/intl/ALL_us/jamboard/

61. Google Keeps (reminders). It enables learners to write a note, edit it, and set a reminder for their due assignments.

62. Google Slides enables teachers to prepare professional slides.

63. Google Books is a great source for books.

64. https://www.chatpdf.com/ is an important website if teachers are researching a topic to gather information.

It saves teachers time by summarizing the content of any PDF document.

65. https://www.chatba.com/ Teachers can upload any file or write a title for any topic, and the website generates slides.

66. https://app.schoolai.com. Great platform that includes great teaching tools to assist teachers. It generates lesson plans, course plans, worksheets on any subject or topic, quizzes with different question styles on any topic, jokes to engage learners, individualized education programs, behavior intervention plans, newsletters to share class updates, generate goals, rubrics, time-based activities, story word problems for any topic, text difficulty levels, allows downloading all documents, text translation to many languages, generates vocabulary based on a subject or topic, and PLC agenda.

67. https://www.brainpop.com/ (with a subscription) is a great source for games on grammar and all language skills.

68. www.tophat.com (with a subscription) powered by AI, this website empowers teachers and learners to create quizzes, polls, discussions, exams, assignments, and personalizable content.

69. https://www.pbslearningmedia.org It has a great resource on all four language skills with videos.

70. https://tools.fobizz.com.

71. https://visuwords.com/. This website gives users a word grid of synonyms for any word they choose.

72. https://www.visualthesaurus.com/ It gives users all the synonyms of a chosen word.

73. https://mindmapmaker.org/ provides options to create a mind map.

74. https://edpuzzle.com/. To store videos and assign them to certain students. It also has many videos with questions in them.

75. https://www.wooclap.com/ It is great to create questions and presentations, collaborate, and view reports.

76. https://app.writecream.com. It creates activities, article writing, paragraph generators, instructions in bullets, photo generators, voiceovers, summaries, headline generators, and blogs for you. It also has paraphraser and plagiarism checker features.

77. https://www.canva.com/p/createclassroommagic/ It has so many templates, designs, and import files.

78. https://www.colorincolorado.org/teaching-english-language-learners nice collection.

79. https://www.schrockguide.net/digital-storytelling.html to create new content.

80. https://www.englishcurrent.com/teachers/

81. Eduaide.AI: Instruction by Design has best practice models for teachers.

GAMIFICATION

Gamification in ESL teaching can transform the learning experience, making it more engaging, motivating, and effective. By incorporating game elements, teachers can create a dynamic and interactive environment that fosters language acquisition, makes lessons more interactive, captures students' attention, and keeps them engaged throughout the learning process. Games not only enhance social interaction, cultural exposure, and inclusivity, but they also create personalized learning and reduce learning anxiety (Pham, 2023).

Games have discussion prompts, review questions, and taxonomy scaffolding (remembering, understanding, applying, analyzing, evaluating, and creating). It generates questions: multiple choices, deep questions, reading comprehension assignments, T/F, matching, team-based activities, engaging activities, and prior knowledge scaffolding. It includes puzzle and trivia-style games, role-playing, and bingo games. It has slideshows and multimedia presentations for goal outlines that are Specific, Measurable, Achievable, Relevant, and Time-Bound (S.M.A.R.T.). It prompts Think-Pair-Share, which utilizes cooperation to improve learner engagement and learning outcomes. The following are some useful websites to reach these goals:

1. https://games4esl.com. It has video activities, PowerPoint games, quizzes, vocabulary and grammar activities, PowerPoint lessons, and vocabulary lists.

2. https://education.minecraft.net/ The games on this website require multiplayer. There are many activities in the curriculum that facilitate personalization.

3. https://www.ego4u.com/en/chill-out/games great collection.

4. https://presenter.ahaslides.com/apps Great games.

5. https://www.eslgamesplus.com/ has great fun games on many grammatical points and vocabulary.

6. https://www.onestopenglish.com/grammar/dominoes-since-and-for/550062.article It has games on many different grammatical points.

7. https://calp.ca/express/word-games.html It has a nice collection of online games.

8. https://www.merriam-webster.com/games is a great source for different games for words, grammar, and quizzes.

9. https://www.gamestolearnenglish.com/ It provides games on various topics, vocabulary, and phrases.

10. https://www.teach-this.com. It is not free, but it has a nice reservoir of great funny game collections.

11. https://civilization.2k.com/civ-iii/ This is a series of games, starting from Civilization I to VI. Learners

should have a basic knowledge of both geography and money, as they are required to build a great society that provides all the necessities for its citizens. The game fosters engagement among learners to build their critical thinking and problem-solving skills.

12. https://www.ubisoft.com/en-us/game/valiant-hearts blends historical facts with engaging storytelling in a WWIII setting so that learners can get a comprehensive idea of this historical event to build their emotional intelligence.

13. https://dragonbox.com/ is an interactive puzzle with challenges to acquire critical thinking and problem-solving skills.

14. https://www.kerbalspaceprogram.com/games-kerbal-space-program has simulation games that let students design, manage, and launch their missions so they acquire decision-making and critical thinking skills.

15. https://worldofwarcraft.blizzard.com/en-us/   It provides games that enhance teaching strategy and collaboration among learners.

16. https://www.tefl.net/elt/ideas/games/15-classroom-language-games/ It has games for the ESL classes and games on grammar.

17. https://eslactive.com/games. It has games on grammar and vocabulary

18. https://www.educaplay.com/. It has many nice plays.

19. https://scratch.mit.edu/ It has many games, and users can create the game with tutorials.

20. https://www.gimkit.com/. Games

21. www.taboo-ai.com The game gives learners an object to describe with a few words not to use (taboos) and checks learners' abilities to help the audience guess the object.

22. https://dashboard.blooket.com/ It has various games.

23. https://www.wordsmyth.net/?mode=activities

24. https://www.topics-mag.com/category/games/

25. https://www.wordsmyth.net/?mode=activities&wl id=w4 It has so nice games and word activities in different levels.

26. https://www.playfactile.com

27. https://www.peardeck.com/ It has many games on different levels.

28. https://www.riddle.com/. (with subscription). It has a very nice collection.

29. https://www.esl-lab.com

30. https://quizizz.com/ Learners join with their mobiles to answer questions.

31. https://www.education.com/game/rebus-reading-comprehension/ It has games on reading comprehension and grammar with different topics and levels of difficulty.

32. https://crosswords.brightsprout.com/crossword-puzzle-maker It enables teachers to create exercises and publish it online so that others can see.

33. https://www.education.com/worksheet-generator/reading/crossword-puzzle/

34. https://crosswordlabs.com/

35. https://wordwall.net/ is great for creating crossword

36. https://worksheets.theteacherscorner.net/make-your-own/crossword/

37. https://monkeylearn.com/word-cloud/. It generates word salad and scrambled words to help learners form a paragraph.

38. https://myfreebingocards.com/ It generates bingo cards for so many topics and enables teachers to call the numbers.

39. https://www.flippity.net/ It is not a free resource. It creates flashcards for a trivia game show, a random name picker or groups, and a randomizing wheel. It creates an interactive virtual board game, as I'm just checking on her health breakout. It also creates a set of click-and-drag objects, tile-matching games, and tic-tac-toe games to illustrate some points. It has bingo games to create interactive timelines. It also creates a typing speed tester; it generates spelling words as teachers are not too busy; word searches; crossword puzzles; word scrambles; and tournament tickets.

40. https://www.abcya.com/ It has some free games, but the majority are premium. However, most of the games are for a very low CLB.

41. https://www.learningchocolate.com/ is a great source for vocabulary on many topics. Each game has four levels: matching, filling, writing the word, and matching the pronunciation of the word with the picture.

42. https://www.spellingcity.com/. It has a lot of courses of games in different parts of the language.
43. https://poki.com/en/quiz. There are so many educational games.
44. https://www.ducksters.com/games/ has great educational games on many topics.
45. https://www.educaplay.com/ is a great source of educational games.
46. https://www.smarttech.com/en/lumio/ has more games.
47. https://gamemaker.io/en/ is a great app for creating games (with subscription).
48. https://www.sandbox.game/en/create/ is a great app for creating video games (with subscription).
49. https://www.jeopardy.com/ has nice game collections.
50. https://jeopardylabs.com/ It allows users to build their games.
51. https://www.crazygames.com/. This website provides collections of games on different topics.
52. https://www.britannica.com/quiz/guess-the-game-quiz has nice games for vocabulary, dictation, names of things, and synonyms.
53. https://www.funnygames.org/. has very nice games in different ways.
54. https://fantasygamesguru.com/ is a great source for games.
55. https://gamestarmechanic.com/ has a nice collection of games.

56. https://www.education.com/ has a great collection of games and activities to practice.
57. https://www.studystack.com/. It enables teachers to create stacks and give crosswords, quizzes, tests, and matching.
58. https://www.typing.com/teacher/ This website enables teachers to get lots of games to type on.
59. https://www.howtopronounce.com/quiz. It is great at creating quizzes on grammar, plus it gives the definitions and pronunciation of words.
60. https://www.englishclub.com/esl-games/vocabulary/ has games on grammar, vocabulary, animals, and more.
61. https://www.blooket.com/ It has a nice collection of games.
62. https://www.digipuzzle.net/education/ It has a great collection of educational games.
63. https://presenter.ahaslides.com/. has a great collection of games.
64. https://www.baamboozle.com/. (With a subscription). Users get great collections of games.
65. https://www.pogo.com/games/trivial-pursuit-online/
66. https://www.internetgames365.com/board-games/
67. https://www.improvememory.org/brain-games/
68. https://thewordsearch.com/ It has great collections of word searches and the feature of a word search maker.
69. https://www.flashcardmachine.com/flashcards/?topic_id=3845482 It has a great collection of flashcards on different topics.

70. https://www.wisc-online.com/search?search Type=2&t=Name&d=Ascending. It is a great source of different games.

71. https://www.playfactile.com/kkz181f3j. It is a great source of games.

72. https://en.bab.la/games/ It is a great source of games.

73. https://api.razzlepuzzles.com/wordsearch It offers many puzzles and word searches on various levels.

74. https://word-search-puzzles.appspot.com/ Word search puzzles as well.

75. https://www.247wordsearch.com/

76. https://puzzlemaker.discoveryeducation.com/. To create crosswords, scrambled sentences, mazes, and word searches.

77. https://www.arkadium.com/games/

78. https://www.classtools.net/ It is a great source of games.

79. https://www.funtrivia.com/quiz/. It is great as it has a great collection of games, quizzes, and various topics.

80. https://www.randomtriviagenerator.com/ It has many games on history, art, geography, and linguistics.

81. https://www.kids.niehs.nih.gov/games It has a nice collection of games for beginners.

82. https://www.npr.org/sections/gaming/ It has nice collections of games.

83. https://triviamaker.com/. It allows teachers to create games and launch them on various topics in English and other subjects.

84. https://www.esl-lounge.com/student/

85.   https://www.rd.com/article/brain-games-quizzes-puzzles/#button-2 It has a great game collection.

86.   https://www.pbslearningmedia.org/subjects/english-language-arts-and-literacy/?rank by=recency   It provides resources for classroom activities.

87.   https://www.taleblazer.org/ Using augmented reality (AR) software, TaleBlazer allows users to play and create their own location-based AR games. In this game, actual landscapes are blended with information from the digital world to create an immersive experience.

88.   http://www.aic.conflix.org/ It provides free games to provide authentic problem-solving in politics.

89.   https://education.mit.edu/project-type/games/ It is a rich site that provides a lot of games on different levels.

90.   https://www.ted.com/talks/jane mcgonigal gaming can make a better word It is a very useful talk on the importance of using games in the classroom.

91.   https://tophat.com/ (for purchase) It offers support and assistance for gamifying curriculum.

92.   https://worldofwarcraft.blizzard.com/en-us/   (for purchase) It is one of the most popular games that helps student engagement.

93.   www.Lensa.ai It turns photos into avatars in different styles.

94.   www.perplexity.ai It provides reliable and accurate answers with citations.

95. www.otter.ai It records meetings and transcribes audio, takes notes, captures slides, and generates summaries.

96. www.starry.ai It generates compositions by describing desired images.

97. www.Socratic.ai is powered by Google to give users the best online resources. Users can use their voice or camera or upload a file. It also provides feedback.

98. www.replika.ai. Makes talking easy and fun.

99. https://www.education.com/lesson-plans/ela/

100. https://ca.ixl.com/ela

101. https://www.popai.pro/. Creates PowerPoint from any uploaded file, creates a chat and presentation with bullets to summarize the file, rewrite it, or choose the audience. Teachers can add pictures or create flowcharts.

102. https://www.smart-words.org/ introduces new vocabulary in various fields with their definitions, synonyms and antonyms.

103. https://diffusionart.co/ &. https://lucidpic.com/ https://dezgo.com/. https://animeart.studio/. It turns text into pictures.

104. https://www.popplet.com/ It provides features to create a poppet and write on it to help with presentations.

105. https://www.onestopenglish.com/ It has a lot of tools to help teachers.

106. https://www.englishcurrent.com/games/

AI FOR CREATING STORYTELLING

Incorporating storytelling into ESL teaching creates a rich, dynamic learning environment that fosters language acquisition, cultural awareness, social and emotional learning, and critical thinking skills. It makes learning more engaging and meaningful, helping students connect with the language on a deeper level. Digital storytelling promotes collaborative learning as learners solve problems and bounce ideas off one another. It improves their writing and presentation skills and provides meaningful ways to learn technology. Below are some useful websites to achieve this target.

1. https://www.storywizard.ai/ It creates stories and can read them aloud, with the possibility of publishing them even on Amazon. Teachers Hub enables teachers to create assignments, including the vocabulary and tense the teacher wants, and then the app will generate a code that students will use to create the story on their own. The teacher can track their progress and download their work as a PDF file.

2. https://remover.zmo.ai/ It enables users to remove any unwanted feature in the image.

3. https://www.writecream.com It enables teachers and students to generate a 1000-word story about any topic. It can over voice it with any voice the user chooses. It turns sentences into instruction patterns.

4. https://pikalabsai.org/ = https://pika.art. It turns any text into videos for free; however, it creates a 3S video, and upgrading is available for longer videos.

5. www.fotor.com To generate pictures of any topic.

6. https://app.pfpmaker.com. For a profile picture.

7. https://convertio.co. It turns any audio, video, or photo into any other format.

8. https://starryai.com/app/my-creations To create images for your story.

9. https://www.onlineocr.net/ It is good to convert all kinds of files into different extensions.

10. www.videolink2me.ai. This app is like Zoom.

11. https://www.english-zone.com It turns any word into a story.

12. https://www.storybird.ai/ It creates a story about any topic. It uses sci-fi, fantasy, etc.

13. https://app.pixton.com/. It is a great resource for presenting comic lessons, comic storytelling, and assessments. It allows users to create comic characters, stories, staff memories, and avatars. It offers different topics for different levels and subjects.

14. https://studio.polotno.com/ It has the same features as Canva, as users can add or adjust photos, upload texts, and adjust fonts.
15. https://www.schrockguide.net/digital-storytelling
16. https://storylineonline.net/ It has a lot of stories illustrated through YouTube.
17. https://boomwriter.com/ It is a great tool to turn students into publishers. Students read one chapter of a story, then, using their imagination, everyone writes the following chapter. Using peer review, students vote for the best chapter and announce the winner who can publish the newly imagined chapter to the story. At the end of this circle, the school prints this book for the children to boost their motivation.
18. https://app.bookcreator.com/ It is a great app for creating a book with pictures.
19. https://www.jasper.ai/ It offers this handy AI art that allows you to easily convert text and images to beautiful art. Jasper offers tools such as mood, medium, inspiration, style, and keywords. Great at advertisements as well.
20. https://deepai.org/ It turns text into speech and generates images and videos from the text and/or pictures.
21. https://www.fotor.com/. AI image generator, background remover, and image editing.
22. https://creator.nightcafe.studio/ It generates images.

23.   https://openai.com/ One of the paid features of Chat GPT is the DALL-E feature, which takes thoughts or all kinds of imagination and turns them into pictures.

24.   https://www.easel.ly/ It provides tools for making bar charts, movies, texts, and graphs with various backgrounds.

25.   https://www.classtools.net/ This website provides a fictitious Facebook and social media account.

References

Abdul Razak, R., Mat Yusoff, S., Hai Leng, C., & Mohamad Marzaini, A. F. (2023). Evaluating teachers' pedagogical content knowledge in implementing classroom-based assessment: A case study among ESL secondary school teachers in Selangor, Malaysia. *PloS One, 18*(12), e0293325-e0293325. https://doi.org/10.1371/journal.pone.0293325

Abucayon, R. L., Mordeno, I. G., Lipa, M. L., Hegakit, M. R., & Manlangit, C. A. S. (2023). Examining the role of technology-supported teaching under the lens of theory of planned behavior. *North American Journal of Psychology, 25*(4), 783-802.

Alberola-Mulet, I., Iglesias-Martínez, M. J., & Lozano-Cabezas, I. (2021). Teachers' beliefs about the role of digital educational resources in educational practice: *A qualitative study. Education Sciences*, 11(5), 239. https://doi.org/10.3390/educsci11050239

Alkhaldi, A. A. (2023). The impact of technology on students' creative writing: A case study in Jordan. *Theory and*

Practice in Language Studies, 13(3), 586-592. https://doi.org/10.17507/tpls.1303.06

Avidov-Ungar, O., & Shamir-Inbal, T. (2017). ICT Coordinators' TPACK-based Leadership Knowledge in their Roles as Agents of Change. *Journal of Information Technology Education, 16,* 169–188. https://doi.org/10.28945/3699

Aziz, S. (2023). Towards a more effective second language writing pedagogy: Using task-based reading to develop writing skills of ESL learners. *University of Chitral Journal of Linguistics and Literature, 5*(I) https://doi.org/10.33195/m7ky0s63

Becuwe, H., Roblin, N. P., Tondeur, J., Thys, J., Castelein, E., & Voogt, J. (2017). Conditions for the successful implementation of teacher educator design teams for ICT integration: A Delphi study. *Australasian Journal of Educational Technology, 33*(2), 159-172. https://doi.org/10.14742/ajet.2789

Bernacki, M. L., Greene, J. A., & Crompton, H. (2020). Mobile technology, learning, and achievement: Advances in understanding and measuring the role of mobile technology in education. *Contemporary Educational Psychology, 60,* 101827. https://doi.org/10.1016/j.cedpsych.2019.101827

Chen, L., & Zhang, J. (2022). Exploring the role and practice of teacher leaders in professional learning communities in China: A case study of a Shanghai secondary school. *Educational Studies, ahead-of-print(ahead-of-print),* 1-19. https://doi.org/10.1080/03055698.2022.2026297

Curran, V., Gustafson, D. L., Simmons, K., Lannon, H., Wang, C., Garmsiri, M., Fleet, L., & Wetsch, L. (2019). Adult learners' perceptions of self-directed learning and digital technology usage in continuing professional education: An update for the digital age. *Journal of Adult and Continuing Education*, 25(1), 74-93. https://doi.org/10.1177/1477971419827318

De León, L., Corbeil, R., & Corbeil, M. E. (2021). The development and validation of a teacher education digital literacy and digital pedagogy evaluation. *Journal of Research on Technology in Education*, 1-13. https://doi.org/10.1080/15391523.2021.1974988

Dorrington, J. (2018). A new organizational architecture to support personalized learning: Parent's perspectives on the academic advisers. *Issues in Educational Research*, 28(2), 349. 366

Ekberg, S., & Gao, S. (2018). Understanding challenges of using ICT in secondary schools in Sweden from teachers' perspective. *The International Journal of Information and Learning Technology*, 35(1), 43-55. https://doi.org/10.1108/IJILT-01-2017-0007

Fadda, H. A., Afzaal, M., & Fadda, N. A. (2020). International standards for E-learning ESL programs: A comparative study. *Revista Argentina De Clínica Psicológica*, 29(5), 174. https://doi.org/10.24205/03276716.2020.1018

Falloon, G. (2020). From digital literacy to digital competence: The teacher digital competency (TDC) framework. *Educational Technology Research and Development*,

68(5), 2449-2472. https://doi.org/10.1007/s11423-020-09767-4

Gomez, F. C., Trespalacios, J., Hsu, Y., & Yang, D. (2021). Exploring teachers' technology integration self-efficacy through the 2017 *ISTE standards. Tech-trends,* 1-13. https://doi.org/10.1007/s11528-021-00639-z

Han, Z. (2022). Digital language learning and SLA. *Bilingualism (Cambridge, England), 25*(3), 388-389. https://doi.org/10.1017/S1366728921000778

Hankins, K. E., & Nicholas, M. (2018). Digital literacies in middle years classrooms: Teachers' perspectives and self-reported practices. *International Journal of Learning,* 24(1), 13-33. https://doi.org/10.18848/1447-9494/CGP/v24i01/13-33

Hicks, S., & Bose, D. (2019). Designing teacher preparation courses: Integrating mobile technology, program standards, and course outcomes. *Techtrends,* 63(6), 734-740. https://doi.org/10.1007/s11528-019-00416-z

Honey, S. (2018). Graphics Calculators in the Primary Classroom: Student-Teachers' Beliefs and the TPACK Framework. *The International Journal for Technology in Mathematics Education,* 25(3), 3-16. https://doi.org/10.1564/tme_v25.3.01

Huang, F., Teo, T., & Zhou, M. (2019). Factors affecting Chinese English as a foreign language teachers' technology acceptance: A qualitative study. *Journal of Educational Computing Research,* 57(1), 83-105. https://doi.org/10.1177/0735633117746168

Ifinedo, P. (2017). Examining students' intention to continue using blogs for learning: Perspectives from technology acceptance, motivational, and social-cognitive frameworks. *Computers in Human Behavior, 72,* 189-199. https://doi.org/10.1016/j.chb.2016.12.049

Jagirani, T. S., Hassan, M., & Ullah, S. (2019). Integrating computer-assisted language learning into ESL classroom: Perception of ESL teachers. *Kuwait Chapter of Arabian Journal of Business & Management Review,* 8(3), 1-11. https://doi.org/10.12816/0054681

Jia, F., Sun, D., Ma, Q., & Looi, C. (2022). Developing an AI-based learning system for L2 learners' authentic and ubiquitous learning in the English language. *Sustainability, 14*(23), 15527. https://doi.org/10.3390/su142315527

Joo, Y. J., Park, S., & Lim, E. (2018). Factors influencing preservice teachers' intention to use. technology: TPACK, teacher self-efficacy, and technology acceptance model. *Educational Technology & Society,* 21(3), 48-59. https://www.jstor.org/stable/26458506

Kambouri, M., Simon, H., & Brooks, G. (2023). Using speech-to-text technology to empower young writers with special educational needs. *Research in Developmental Disabilities, 135,* 104466-104466. https://doi.org/10.1016/j.ridd.2023.104466

Kearney, M., Schuck, S., & Burden, K. (2022). Digital pedagogies for future school education: Promoting inclusion. *Irish Educational Studies, 41*(1), 117-133. https://doi.org/10.1080/03323315.2021.2024446

Lee, Y., & Martin, K. I. (2020). The Flipped classroom in ESL Teacher education: An example from CALL. *Education and Information Technologies*, 25(4), 2605-2633. https://doi.org/10.1007/s10639-019-10082-6

Li, K. L., Razali, A. B., Noordin, N., Samad, A. A., & Universiti Putra Malaysia, M. (2018). The role of digital technologies in facilitating the learning of ESL writing among TESL pre-service teachers in Malaysia: A review of the literature. *Journal of Asia TEFL, 15*(4), 1139-1145. https://doi.org/10.18823/asiatefl.2018.15.4.18.1139

Li, R. (2023). Effects of mobile-assisted language learning on EFL learners' listening skill development. *Educational Technology & Society, 26*(2), 36-49. https://doi.org/10.30191/ETS.202304_26(2).0003

Liu, H., Lin, C., Zhang, D., & Zheng, B. (2018). Chinese language teachers' perceptions of technology and instructional use of technology: A path analysis. *Journal of Educational Computing Research*, 56(3), 396-414. https://doi.org/10.1177/0735633117708313

Mariappan, R., Tan, K. H., Yang, J., Chen, J., & Chang, P. K. (2022). Synthesizing the attributes of computer-based error analysis for ESL and EFL learning: A scoping review. *Sustainability, 14*(23), 15649. https://doi.org/10.3390/su142315649

Martin, A. J., Mansour, M., & Malmberg, L. (2020). What factors influence students' real-time motivation and engagement? an experience sampling study of high school students using mobile technology. *Educational*

Psychology (Dorchester-on-Thames), 40(9), 1113-1135. https://doi.org/10.1080/01443410.2018.1545997

Marzuki, Widiati, U., Rusdin, D., Darwin, & Indrawati, I. (2023). The impact of AI writing tools on the content and organization of students' writing: EFL teachers' perspective. *Cogent Education, 10*(2)https://doi.org/10. 1080/2331186X.2023.2236469

Muftah, M. (2023). Data-driven learning (DDL) activities: Do they truly promote EFL students' writing skills development? *Education and Information Technologies, 28*(10), 13179-13205. https://doi.org/10.1007/s10639-023-11620-z

Ndlovu, M., Ramdhany, V., Spangenberg, E. D., & Govender, R. (2020). Preservice teachers' beliefs and intentions about integrating mathematics teaching and learning ICTs in their classrooms. *Zdm,* 52(7), 1365-1380. https://doi.org/10.1007/s11858-020-01186-2

Nordlof, C., Hallstrom, J., & Host, G. E. (2019). Self-efficacy or context-dependency?: Exploring teachers' perceptions of and attitudes towards technology education. *International Journal of Technology and Design Education,* 29(1), 123-141. https://doi.org/10.1007/s10798-017-9431-2

Peungcharoenkun, T., & Waluyo, B. (2023). Implementing process-genre approach, feedback, and technology in L2 writing in higher education. *Asian-Pacific Journal of Second and Foreign Language Education, 8*(1), 34-20. https://doi.org/10.1186/s40862-023-00211-7

Pham, A. T. (2023). The impact of gamified learning using quizizz on ESL learners' grammar achievement.

Contemporary Educational Technology, 15(2), ep410. https://doi.org/10.30935/cedtech/12923

Poth, R. D. (2019). Teacher education network activities for ISTE 2019. *Journal of Digital Learning in Teacher Education, 35*(2), 74-75. https://doi.org/10.1080/2153 2974.2019.1592412

Pourhosein Gilakjani, A., & Rahimy, R. (2020). Using computer-assisted pronunciation teaching (CAPT) in English pronunciation instruction: A study on the impact and the Teacher's role. *Education and Information Technologies, 25*(2), 1129-1159. https://doi.org/10.1007/ s10639-019-10009-1

Rahman, M. M., PhD, Jamila, M., & Md Mahmudur Rahman Siam. (2024). Language skills development: EFL teachers' and learners' perceptions of the existing Teaching– Learning practices. *The International Journal of Literacies, 32*(1), 1. https://doi.org/10.18848/2327-0136/ CGP/v32i01/1-20

Raman, A., & Thannimalai, R. (2019). Importance of technology leadership for technology integration: Gender and professional development perspective. *SAGE* Open, 9(4), 215824401989370. https://doi. org/10.1177/2158244019893707

Reamer, F. G. (2019). Social work education in a digital world: Technology standards for education and practice. *Journal of Social Work Education, 55*(3), 420-432. https://doi.or g/10.1080/10437797.2019.1567412

Regan, K., Evmenova, A. S., Sacco, D., Schwartzer, J., Chirinos, D. S., & Hughes, M. D. (2019). Teacher perceptions of integrating technology in writing. Technology, *Pedagogy and Education*, 28(1), 1-19. https://doi.org/10.1080/147 5939X.2018.1561507

Rodriguez-Gomez, D., Castro, D., & Meneses, J. (2018). Problematic uses of ICT among young people in their personal and school life. *Comunicar*, 26(56), 91-100. https://doi.org/10.3916/C56-2018-09

Sadaf, A., & Johnson, B. L. (2017). Teachers' beliefs about integrating digital literacy into classroom practice: An investigation based on the theory of planned behavior. *Journal of Digital Learning in Teacher Education*, 33(4), 129-137. https://doi.org/10.1080/21532974.2017.1 347534

Scherer, R., Siddiq, F., & Tondeur, J. (2019). The technology acceptance model (TAM): A meta-analytic structural equation modeling approach to explaining teachers' adoption of digital technology in education. *Computers and Education*, 128, 13-35. https://doi.org/10.1016/j. compedu.2018.09.009

Schmid, R., Pauli, C., Stebler, R., Reusser, K., & Petko, D. (2022). Implementation of technology-supported personalized learning-its impact on instructional quality. *The Journal of Educational Research (Washington, D.C.)*, 115(3), 187-198. https://doi.org/10.1080/00220 671.2022.2089086

Siefert, B., Kelly, K., Yearta, L., & Oliveira, T. (2019). Teacher perceptions and use of technology across content areas with linguistically diverse middle school students. *Journal of Digital Learning in Teacher Education*,

35(2), 107-121. https://doi.org/10.1080/21532974.201
9.1568327

Singh, C. K. S., Singh, H. K. S., Singh, T. S. M., Tek, O.
E., Yunus, M. M., Rahmayanti, H., & Ichsan, I. Z.
(2021). Review of research on the use of audio-visual
aids among learners' English language. *Turkish Journal
of Computer and Mathematics Education, 12*(3), 895-
904. https://doi.org/10.17762/turcomat.v12i3.800

Uiboleht, K., Karm, M., & Postareff, L. (2019). Relations
between students' perceptions of the teaching-learning
environment and teachers' approaches to teaching:
A qualitative study. *Journal of further and Higher
Education,* 43(10), 1456-1475. https://doi.org/10.1080
/0309877X.2018.1491958

Uzumcu, O., & Bay, E. (2021). The effect of computational
thinking skill program design developed according to
interest is driven creator theory on prospective teachers.
Education and Information Technologies, 26(1), 565-
583. https://doi.org/10.1007/s10639-020-10268- 3

Voithofer, R., Nelson, M. J., Han, G., & Caines, A. (2019).
Factors that influence TPACK adoption by teacher
educators in the US. *Educational Technology Research
and Development,* 67(6), 1427-1453. https://doi.
org/10.1007/s11423-019-09652-9

Wan, A., & Ivy, J. (2021). Providing access by integrating
computer-aided design in mathematics teacher
education courses. *Journal of Digital Learning in Teacher
Education,* 1-13. https://doi.org/10.1080/21532974.202
1.1965506

Xu, S., Yang, H. H., MacLeod, J., & Zhu, S. (2019). Interpersonal communication competence and digital citizenship among pre-service teachers in China's teacher preparation programs. *Journal of Moral Education*, 48(2), 179-198. https://doi.org/10.1080/03057240.2018.1458605

Zhang, J., Chen, Z., Ma, J., & Liu, Z. (2021). Investigating the influencing factors of teachers' information and communications technology-integrated teaching behaviors toward "Learner-centered" reform using structural equation modelling. *Sustainability*, 13(22), 12614. https://doi.org/10.3390/su132212614

Zhen, L. S., & Hashim, H. (2022). The usage of MALL in learners' readiness to speak English. *Sustainability*, *14*(23), 16227. https://doi.org/10.3390/su142316227

Zhong, L. (2017). Indicators of digital leadership in the context of K-12 education. *Journal of Educational Technology Development and Exchange*, 10 (1) https://doi.org/10.18785/jetde.1001.03

Printed in the United States
by Baker & Taylor Publisher Services